The Ultimate Advantage

The Art of Self-Promotion:
Master
Your Time, Your Money,
Your Power

4-24-15

Cheryl!

Enjoy this book

Prov 31:10

Daniel Ally

Excerpt as permitted under the United States Copyright Act of 1976, no part of this publication may be reproduced and distributed in any form or by any means, or stored in a data base or retrieval system, without the prior written permission of the publisher.

The Ally Way

International
www.danielally.com
info@danielally.com

The Ultimate Advantage. Copyright © 2014 Daniel A. Ally
Printed and Manufactured in the United States of America.
All rights reserved.

Dignify Designs Publications
www.dignifydesigns.com
info@dignifydesigns.com

ISBN-10: 1500474800
ISBN-13: 978-1500474805

10 9 8 7 6 5 4 3 2 1

This is dedicated to those who are ready to be audacious, contagious, and tenacious.

Introduction

In just a few years, I went from being over $250,000 in debt, a purposeless substance abuser in his mother's basement, and a man who was living far below his potential to eventually becoming a two-time published author, highly-demanded consultant, superstar speaker and trainer with a multitude of Fortune 500 companies---all by the age of 24.

It seems almost impossible to think that I went from failing several classes and delivering a sub-par performance at work to getting straight A's, starting two businesses, and writing two books straight out of college! How did I go from playing video games and basketball for hours to reading hundreds of books and giving 500 speeches, all within two years?

How can someone like myself escape the poverty and welfare system in New York City to eventually inspiring thousands of people per week? I used to be habitually late to every event. It took me an hour before I got out of bed, but now I spring out of bed and you will see that I am early every time. I cursed angrily and I couldn't even look people firmly in the eyes, nor could I say my name confidently, but now my words can paint a portrait faster than a street performer. Where did this come from?

Instead of watching television and listening to overplayed songs on the radio, I am regularly on television and radio. Women and jobs avoided me at all cost in the past, but now they flow steadily to me, even though I do not need them. I went from an overweight kid to a robustly muscular man. How did all of this happen?

People made fun of me in my old Volkswagen Beetle for years, but when I drove past some of them with my new Mercedes-Benz, they quickly asked me to forgive them and searched for a way for reconciliation. I went from wearing cargo shorts and t-shirts with sandals to having a full wardrobe of wool suits, silk ties, and pretty shoes with leather heels. Where did it come from?

When I was working at my current job at age 21, which was at a men's retail store, I went from being the last place in sales to breaking company records. I went from working over 50 hours, to working on appointments. I went from calling on people all day and every day to having people call me all day and every day. I even did business with the governor, several celebrities, and people from out-of-state before I decided to righteously quit my job. I never worked for another person after I mastered that job.

After working over thirty odd jobs in all different industries, I resolved that I would start my own business, even though I was deeply in debt with no ideas how to do business. I did not care what anyone thought, even though I faced plenty of opposition. I was determined that it was time to take charge of my life, it was time to gain The Ultimate Advantage!

I found out quickly how to get promoted in life and work. I learned how to network and speak with authority in public. I would speak 5-10 times per week. I would travel to different states, even when I didn't have money. I faced dozens of toll booths where I had to fish out my last coins or ask the person in the car behind me for help. I had plenty of tickets for parking in the wrong spots in the city just to make the meetings I had to speak at on time. I went on 24 hour days, some without food and obviously with little sleep. I had to go through countless security checkpoints, that I know every code word that they use! I traveled thousands of miles to give hundreds of free speeches.

One time I walked by a homeless person realizing that his net worth was many times more than mine! I steadily paid off my debt as I learn different ways to help people. I explored so many opportunities and failed most of them. I got drenched in rain and drove through a few dozen feet of snow! People thought I was crazy. None of my audiences ever knew what I was going through to help them. I was fully convicted and believed wholeheartedly in what I did. I always felt that God was with me, even through my deepest moments of trial. I think that is why I did what I did. I knew I was living my purpose. There was no question about it.

By the way, people ask me all the time, "How do I know what my purpose is?" The best way to know is by determining what you consistently think about improving. For instance, if you feel that children need to learn how to read and you feel that you can add value by improving their condition, then that is your purpose. You would want to become an elementary school teacher. Your purpose is what you are truly passionate about, regardless of pay. It is what you are willing to do to help people to improve their situation.

There are dozens of techniques that you can use in this book toward your life that can help you excel. I do recommend that you try at least one per week or until it becomes a habit. There are some that may not work for you. My goal is for you to find at least one that will dramatically change your life. If you find more than one, all the better. Study this book diligently and take notes. With the tools in this book, you will be able to make changes in your life once you learn that you too have The Ultimate Advantage! Enjoy...

Write Your Goals

Your goals must be written down on paper. Let's take an example of a goal and learn the recipe to set it:

Today's Date: January 1st, 2015

Specific Goal: Earn $300,000 at my Residential Real Estate Job by January 1st, 2017

Goal term: 2 Years

Action steps:

1. Order 5 books per month for 2 years via Amazon.com to obtain 120 books
2. Get books on sales, real estate, marketing, time-management, leadership, vocabulary, etc.
3. Separate them according to genre
4. Network 2 times per month
5. Make 500 sales calls per month
6. Talk to industry leaders once per month

7. Attend 4 sales seminars per year
8. Practice presentation 2 times per week

Of course, you can set many more action steps. You get the idea. The goals must be SMART-Specific, Measureable, Attainable, Relevant, Timely. Use a measuring device to record how well you are doing. Write down your goals every morning or night. Be sure to keep them with you everywhere you go.

To achieve maximum results, write them down twice daily and put sticky notes in your bathroom, bedroom, kitchen, car, and any other dwelling place. Also, laminate your goals and put it in your shower. Put pictures of your goals all over your home. Become infatuated with your goals by believing in it and taking the action steps necessary to achieve it.

When you have a goal, you must be flexible. Things may not work out exactly as you have planned. Make room for changes. Your mind will also change and certain things will happen in your life. New opportunities will begin to appear. If your priorities seem to change, which is natural, just go with the change.

If you realize that the goal is too high, lower it. A goal that is set too high may discourage you if it is unreasonably unreachable. Setting a goal to be a millionaire in one year is not a realistic goal if you have only earned $60,000 the previous year. A good rule of thumb to increase your income is 1.5-2 times. If you earned $50,000 this year, aim for $75,000-$100,000 by next year. Of course, you can always earn more.

If your goal is too low, bring it up to higher standards. It is normal to raise your goal because you start to see the bigger picture as you go along in your journey. As you start to realize your potential, it is very good to increase the size of your goal. It will only increase your intensity in achieving it.

Goals are the navigational system to get to your destination. When you know where you are going, there will be many opportunities that come along to get you there. People with no goals tend to drift. There is an old saying that goes, "If you do not know where you are going, any road will take you there." It is true. You must know where you are going.

Many people are afraid to set goals because they do not know how it can be attained. Your goal will always be reached if you put the effort and creativity into it. There are also unseen forces that will start to work in your advantage. Things will start to line up because you prepared yourself for these opportunities. Goals lead you into the Law of Expectation. When you expect certain things and situations, they tend to happen, especially when you have faith.

Write and review your goals every day. Expect them to happen. Be eager like a child on the first day of kindergarten. Goals fuel you and will give you that new boost of energy that you never had before. It will make you get up early in the morning. Goals give you an adventure. A person with properly set goals will never be bored in life. Set as many goals as you can and achieve them all. You will be in control of your life and you will have The Ultimate Advantage!

Success Whiteboard

How do you keep track of your success? Do you have a Success Whiteboard? This is a board where you can keep track of your success. You should keep one for the year, month, week, and day. This must be updated every day. It is a very fine tracking device that can be implemented. Get a white panel board from a home improvement store to cut the cost of buying one already made. You can also buy one that is already made online or at retail stores.

One major success rule is "if it isn't measured, it isn't managed." Be your own manager and keep track of your victories. Ensure that your Success Whiteboard's positioning is conducive to your room and its size. Place your major goals on your success whiteboard and look at it often as a reminder.

The best way to do this is to write it on paper, then transfer it to your success whiteboard. Start with your overall yearly goals. Then break it down to individual month. After each month ends, erase and start the next month. Create plans for weeks and days also. There are many ways to do this. Be sure that you have enough whiteboards, markers, and erasers. Keep your markers and your erasers in reach at all times.

Keep it in a private area so that when visitors come by, they do not know how successful you really are. Update the board regularly and keep it interesting and inspirational. Be very methodical and push yourself to reach all of your goals. Put your financial goal at the top and label all categories correctly. You know you are a success when your year board gets messy at the end. Re-write your board if it does get messy. You can also keep a separate whiteboard to brainstorm ideas if you are a spontaneous person. Use this method for strategic thinking and planning. Enjoy your Success Whiteboard. It will give you The Ultimate Advantage!

Tracking Expenses

As mentioned a few pages ago, "What isn't measured isn't managed." It is even truer when it comes to money. You will find that the wealthiest people in this world track all of their expenses, even when they were in debt. You can be sure that this method is not used by the majority of people in the world. Those who do not use this method will live from paycheck to paycheck. You don't want to have too much month at the end of the money.

How do you solve this problem? You can simply keep a small book in your pocket or purse with you at all times to track your expenditures. Every time you purchase something, be sure to write it down. Even if it costs a nickel, record it. You can even be more advanced by keeping track of everything you earned too, if it suits you by using a monthly calendar. When you write it down, make sure you transfer it to a bigger spreadsheet at the end of the week or month. If you want, you can use computer software or an accountant.

People often wonder why they are in financial desperation and always scrambling for money. If you knew where your money actually went, you would not be spending it the way you were in the past. When you record your expenditures, this leaves a subconscious imprint on your mind. The next time you pick up something that you don't need, you will realize that you can put it off for a later date.

When making a big purchase, ask yourself "Do I have to make this purchase within the next 60 days?" When you ask this question, you will decline more than half of the major purchases that often cost you too much. Even the small things can affect you. The $3 coffee that is bought 250 days out of the year is $750. You can make a small investment with that!

Most people keep budgets of what they spend, but they are generally not as specific as they need to be. For instance, they will estimate that they spend $500 a month on food to feed themselves, but the actual cost might be $834.68. The reason they do not want to write down the actual cost of what they spend is because they are afraid of losing the habit that they love and are unwilling to make the personal sacrifice that can pay off handsomely in the long run.

We all work hard for the money we earn and the last thing we want to do is know where it all goes. We simply want to enjoy what we earned. Some of us like to splurge on big parties every other month that can cost thousands of dollars. However, if you are really committed to becoming more wealthy, then you will start writing down your actual expenditures. You want to be more savvy with your income. It is not always about how much you gain, but it is about how much you keep.

If you don't choose to do this, you will keep fooling yourself. At the end of life, you may run into what is called a 'social security' check, pension, or even welfare. Finally, you will start to ask the question, "Where did all the money go?" at the age of 70. You should have known when you were in your 20's. Record your expenses, even if it seems like a hassle. It will be one of the best things that you ever did. This disciplined way of tracking your expenses will give you The Ultimate Advantage!

Reading Books

When you read books, you will begin to shape your thinking. As you read this book, you have begun to learn that there are multiple ways to attain success in life. Reading books gives you fresh ideas so that you can produce more in life. Ideas are the key to developing a winner.

It is best to read a non-fiction book. It is unfortunate that most libraries are filled with fiction novels with detailed stories. You have to cut through all of the junk to get to the point when you read fiction books. If you elect to read non-fiction books, you will find practical tips that will help you become better in the area you choose. Fiction books are good and easy to read, but non-fiction books are better because they challenge your thoughts.

If you chose to read 5-10 books on one subject and really study it carefully, you will have enough knowledge to become a national expert. Because most people read a book or less per month, you will have an edge. Many people will read newspaper, magazines, blogs, and articles to think that they are really learning something. You definitely can learn from these sources, but nothing will be more detailed and focused as a good book on one specific subject. Plus, you can extract many nuances that the author of the book will express.

Wake up with a book in your hand every day and watch how quickly you will grow. If you read at least one hour per day, you will be able to read at least a dozen books per year. To really expand your mind, read one per week. If you read a book every week, you will be able to read at least 50 per year. You will easily become an expert in what you are studying. In fact, you become what you study.

Another skill in reading that should be learned is to read faster. Most people read by subvocalizing. This means that they are saying the words in their minds instead of reading big blocks of words at a time. You can dramatically read books faster by using your finger or hand to guide you. There are so many books that share techniques on rapid reading. You can find many of them on Amazon.com

Reading is the key because it gives you the access to knowledge you did not formerly have. When you read, it forces you to think creatively and challenges your logic. The reason why most people do not read is because they are distracted and sometimes fear to learn the truth. True leaders are readers. When you read, it will unlock you mind in extraordinary ways which will give you The Ultimate Advantage!

Write Daily

Writing everyday can change your speaking, thinking, and writing. A great challenge is to write 1,000 words per day. It will only take an hour at most if you do research on what you want to write about. You can start out with 250 or 500 words a day if you would like and work your way up. You can set any writing goal and achieve it if you want.

Writing helps you recognize and organize your thoughts. It helps you get ideas out and reach epiphanies. Writing will not only help you, but it will help your readers too. If you are in a particular industry, you can share ideas with your colleagues. You can even get many ideas from them. In this world of the internet, you can blog once or twice a week and reach thousands of people per month.

You can even write a book. Every person has a book in them. If you want to write 1,000 words per day, you can create a 150 page book with 30,000 words by the end of 30 days. A typical 200 page book can take up to

40,000 words, which can be written and published in less than two months. Of course, the amount of pages varies depending on how you format your book and what kinds of additional materials you add to it. Contact me at www.danielally.com and I will put you in touch with my personal publisher. She does exceptional work and can help you publish a book in less than a month!

Whether you are writing in your journal, blog, or book, you will release insights and wisdom that you may not have realized you formerly had. This will help you in your work and will help you in your life. It will give you more clarity, depth, and substance in everything you do. When you write, you are sharing your knowledge, which will be multiplied. You learn far more when you write. You can also write manuals, brochures, or any other kind of written materials that can help you and others.

Here is what you can produce by writing 1,000 words per day:

1,000 words X 30 days = 30,000 words per month

30,000 words X 12 months = 360,000 words per year

360,000 words X 45 working years = 16,200,000 words in a lifetime

16,200,000 words= 540 books!!!

Okay, 540 books may seem a bit overwhelming, but I can assure you that you can write a book or two. You have stories, ideas, principles, values, wisdom, and experience that no one else can ever have. You do not have to be a full-time writer, but a little writing on the side can give you a quantum leap in your life. This can be for your own satisfaction and/or the benefit of others. Writing is one of the most powerful ways of communicating your message. The least you can do it write one book! Go ahead, you can do it. Writing is the basis of all wealth and will give you The Ultimate Advantage!

Journal

Keeping a daily record of what you are doing allows you access your progression. It allows you to keep track of your past to help you make adjustments in the future. You can then review what you have written and learn from that time in which you have lived. When you look in the past, you will find that you have changed quite a bit, because there is no way you would do what you did before.

When certain things happen in your life, you must record it. You may see something extraordinary or feel a certain way about a situation. When you write it down, it will help you think about what is happening and can actually help you resolve your problem. A brilliant thought can instantly vanish if you do not take the opportunity to write it down in your journal. Keep your journal with you at all times.

A journal can also be a good tool for 'reflection' in the future. When you look back and see how far you have come and what you have done, this allows you to reflect and see where you were in the past and how far you have gotten. You will be able to cherish it as long as you live. Without it being written down, you will have forgotten about it and no one would be likely to remind you of that particular event.

Looking back allows you to review from your mistakes, recognize what you have learned, and reminisce over the times you once had. With a journal, you can record jokes, stories, ideas, philosophies, events, people, music that you like, quotes, books, and all sorts of information and facts all in a bound version. You can also categorize your journal according to your specifications.

Many people write things down in scraps of paper and toss it in their purses or pockets, only to find that this disorganization led to the trash receptacle. A journal captures the very essence of life and allows you to relive all of your experiences in a meaningful way, just as you had before.

It is one of the greatest tool to grow with. Best of all, it is for you and your family to admire in the future. It can also be as personal as you would like it. After all, you probably have your own secrets. It is one of the best ways to remember how great your life is operating. Keeping a journal will also allow your grandchildren to know you better. They will read the stories about you and their imaginations will go wild after they hear about all of your secrets and fantasies. It's different when they heard about your vintage Corvette or bellbottom jeans versus seeing pictures and reading stories about it.

You will be a legend in your family. In ancient times, people would pass down stories or write on the walls of the cave, but today Wal-Mart sells journals for about one dollar. Pens at the bank are free. Take 10-20 minutes every day to record your life. If you get anything out of this whole book, I want you to do this the most.

Keep a journal and know who you are. Keeping inventory of your past can help you better predict what you can do better in the future. In the long run, it is worth the dollars and time you invest. Writing down your thought will keep you sharp and allow you to have The Ultimate Advantage!

Keep a Small Book

How often have you been in the situation where something comes to mind, but you do not have anything to write on? You look around for a pen and there is nothing to write with either. You think to yourself that the idea is important to catch, but you debate finding the tools to catch the idea. By the time you find a pen and a piece of paper, you already lost the idea! This is one of the most tragic things that can happen.

Never be caught without your tools. Always have something to write on and an instrument to write with. Carry a small book in your pocket or purse so that you can write your ideas down. I keep one in my suit pockets at all times. It gives me another reason to wear a suit or blazer every time I go out in public. People will suggest many things and it is imperative that you write it down. Not only will you have the idea, but it will show great respect with those you communicate with. Always have a pen, even if it is a cheap one. Actually, have more than one pen in case one doesn't work. You can also let people borrow your pens as well because you will find that most people don't carry pens on them. Be sure to keep the pen and book accessible so that you don't have to take a minute to fish it out.

When you keep this small book, you can also keep a calendar so that you know when people are talking about particular dates. If you have your schedule in this book, all the better. An advanced technique is to keep notecards and business cards in this book. With the notecards, you can draw out ideas with another or you can give one to another person for them to write on. You will be handing out notecards with people more than you ever think after you notice that they do not have something to write with. When you do it, you have a chance to share this powerful technique with them.

Another advance technique is to keep notecard of your goals in your book. When you are standing in line, waiting for someone or something for some reason, you can easily pop out a notecard of your goals. Throughout the year, you will probably look at this 50-100 times or more, depending on how much you remember the fact that it is actually there. It will dramatically increase your success.

By having the book, it will give you the comfort and security of knowing that you can write down anything that comes to mind. When you go home, you can transfer what you have in your small book into your journal if you would like. Of course, in today's world, you do not have to carry the actual book if you do not want because a smartphone or tablet will suffice.

You will always be safe when you carry the book however. When you get into the habit of writing in it, you will find your mind expanding. You will also be able to remember things. People are always teaching and distributing resources, so you might as well get as many as you can by writing them down. This powerful technique of keeping a small book with goals, a mini calendar, notecards, and a writing instrument will give you The Ultimate Advantage!

Carry a Camera

Picture what can happen when you carry a camera everywhere you go. If you take many pictures throughout your life, you will be able to store all of your memories that words alone cannot utter. When you carry a camera, you can snap a picture of some of the most amazing places, people, and things in your life.

Whether it is a smart phone or a slim pocket camera, always carry a camera everywhere you go. Take pictures of yourself, others, nature, artwork, animals, signs, bodies of water, or anything that seems fascinating. What you are doing is taking a moment to appreciate what you are seeing at the moment.

There are a few things that you leave behind for your family when you are gone from the world. They are your journals, books, furniture, and pictures. When you come home from each adventurous day, upload your pictures and try to develop them at the end of every month. When you are long gone, your family will cherish the great pictures that you took when you were alive.

Hopefully, your pictures will be consistent with what you wrote in your journals!

Also, keep pictures around with materials that you want. If there is a particular car, house, or any other possession that you want, take a picture of it. This will help you visualize it while it comes to fruition in your actual life. You know the old saying, "A picture is worth 1,000 words." I would like to add on to that by saying that 1,000 pictures are worth a million words! Photos can help you build your vision for your future.

Imagine the laughter you and your family will have in the future of you and your endeavors. They will enjoy the cars you drove, the haircuts you kept, and the friends you had. These pictures will be enjoyed from generation to generation. Always be sure to carry a camera everywhere you go. You never know when you will see an unexpected miracle. You can always catch it on camera, but only when you have one!! Carrying a camera will give you The Ultimate Advantage!

Use Social Media

Every day, the internet is changing the way we view the world. Social media has an instrumental role in the internet's development and is one of your greatest vehicles of expression. You can use all kinds of social media, but make sure you are using the right ones for the right reasons.

It would be perfectly acceptable to put a video of your signature mashed potato recipe on Youtube.com, but may not be appropriate on Linkedin.com. You can send all kinds of one-liners on LinkedIn, but it would probably fit better on Facebook or Twitter. You can use almost all of the social media platforms to blog and exchange ideas. Find the right ones for your needs.

The exchange of ideas and expression of yourself should be your main goals for using social media. It shouldn't be a conduit for escaping reality as it has become for millions of people. Many people will take up hours of their day succumbing to the subtle influences of the dominating thoughts of others. They will find themselves glued to what comments are being posted and try to "like" certain materials that has no relevance with their success. This happens because we are curious and want to often get into the action, but it can be deleterious if it prohibits us from using our day effectively.

There are certain social media profiles that are completely filled with trash. Others will send you mail via messages or emails that will consume much of your time. Social media can be a major distraction if you do not understand its proper uses. It is a mode for your self-expression, not drifting toward the willpower of others. You can enjoy your real friends on there too, but there comes a problem when you begin to partake in the wild world of randomness. Stay focused on what you came to do on whatever social media platform that you want to use.

You can even use social media for business, information, and relationship-building purposes. When you start to use it for entertaining purposes, you begin to lose a lot of valuable time. You can also use it to find a spouse or a best friend on the internet using social media. However, that usually happens in a spontaneous way, rather than an intellectually-directed way.

Social media is a powerful tool to gain information. You can also use it to keep in touch with your former relationships or even reach out to people you never met before. Search for profiles that are highly organized, inspirational, and relevant to your success. Be sure to keep safe pictures and content on your profile too.

Many people will search for your online, so be aware of this great fact. Using social media the correctly can help you in many ways. It is almost impossible to evade it entirely in your are on the internet, so use it right. Find the ones that work well for your style and use it. There are dozens to choose from. The right social media usage will give you The Ultimate Advantage!

Traveling

When you travel, you have the great privilege of expanding your mind. It can surprise you on what you can see when you go a few miles outside of your house. It's even more astounding when you travel 3,000 miles from home. Go across the world and you will quickly realize how blessed you really are!

Try to travel to a different state once a month if you live in the United States of America. Strive to go to a different country or two every year. When you do this, you will reach all 50 states and 50 or more countries in a lifetime, depending on when you start. You will see amazing things and meet interesting people that will make you more aware of what is going on in the world. You will also notice that many of the cultural stereotypes that you have heard about in the past will be false.

When you travel, you feel a different atmosphere. You eat a different food and depending on where you are, you use a different system of time, money, and transportation. The music will be different and the eye contact and gestures will make you think about the difference or similarities that you will find in your own culture.

It is always sobering to find that people desire the same things all over the world. Most people want to be healthy, have a good family, and a stable income. Some regions will be different and you will see breathtaking sights. Bring your camera along and be sure to know how to handle the cultural norms. Failure to act according to the standards in another territory can be very awkward and embarrassing, but don't let this stop you from traveling.

You begin to open your mind and receive special wisdom, understanding, and gratitude when you travel. Go and see the open oceans or the vast mountains. Visit the hottest or coldest parts that you can handle in the world. Try to see through the lens of other cultures in the world. Get ready to be surprised. It will be mind-altering, because traveling the world gives you The Ultimate Advantage!

Organize and Clean

Keeping everything organized and clean is one of the major fundamentals that must be taken seriously. Having an organized and clean environment will help you think more clearly and produce the highest results. It will also make your dwelling areas more appealing to you and to those who visit you.

Clean your desk, car, and entire house. Get the dirty spots that build up like the bathrooms, closets, and kitchen. Organize everything neatly and get into the habit of keeping everything clear so that you can easily find all that you would ever need.

It is always profitable to deal with a piece of paper only once. You either must decide to keep it or discard it. Never allow it to pile up. It will only become an extra unnecessary burden. Keep shoes organized too. Make sure your car is always ready to transport passengers, even if you do not normally invite others into your car. Do not keep food anywhere in your home, desk, or car. That is not where you should not be eating. Ensure that your desk only has the work in which you are currently assuming.

Organize your wallet or purse. Keep pens and paper handy in every dwelling area. Books shall be in their proper places and carpets and floors should always be clean. You should know where every important ingredient in your life is located. Never allow clothing to consume areas in your house where it doesn't belong. Find the system of cleaning and organizing that works for you.

Do you have a designated area for your keys? What about your important documents? Your birthday cards? What about your business cards with contacts? Do you just trash them, or do you keep them in an area that you have created? Do you jam everything into your desk drawers? You should be able to navigate freely in your desk and car. Give your desk and car a good cleaning every month. It will be worth your time.

Just like brushing your teeth and taking a shower in a daily fashion, you must habitually organize and clean every area of your life. If you are a hoarder, get someone to help you clear out the islands of buildup. Neglecting your space of living and work will leave you disoriented. Give away the old clothes or anything that unnecessarily takes up room. You will instantly become a better person overall when you begin to organize and clean your environment and your mind. Organizing and cleaning up will give you The Ultimate Advantage!

Pray Often

Prayer is the nourishment that sustains you. When you pray to your Creator, you are admitting your finiteness. You admit that you cannot do more than what you have already done. Prayer helps you to submit and get in touch with a power that is always greater than you.

When you pray, make sure you pray sincere prayers. Pray earnestly and expectantly. Meditate on your prayers. Wait for answers and ask for divine guidance. Ask that you receive wisdom, understanding, ideas, and purpose. Pray for your steps to be directed and for your life to be protected. Pray for that which you desire. Align yourself with the great power of God.

Meditate on the truths that you already know. Affirm it in your mind and obey the Spirit that lives within you. There is always a conscious pull and you can feel it when you pray sincerely. With a deep belief and profound faith, your prayers will be answered if they are righteous and if they pursue love.

You can pray for anything. You can pray for better and stronger relationships, divine guidance, wisdom, truth, greater health, favorite foods, understanding, material good, and everything else. Your prayers put you in contact with the Almighty Power that can give you a deeper connection to what you are praying for.

Prayer must become instinctual. You must become acquainted with the force in which you pray with and heed its calling. You will start to get in touch with God and the World. You will gain more control and leverage your mind. Prayer conditions you to be ready and prepared for any given circumstance. It allows you to get into your mind. It helps you focus on all of your priorities.

Know that your prayers are answered and that they will come to fruition as long as you believe it. They may not appear at your timing, but if they are good prayers, they will appear at the right timing. Pray morning and night. Try to pray 5-10 times per day. They do not have to be long and you do not have to be an expert at praying. There is no one way of doing it and you can learn by practicing and hearing others pray. Start with the word, "Father", then let the rest roll by asking for what you need. This is one of the most powerful forces that you can use and prayer will definitely give you The Ultimate Advantage when you use it right!

Network

Connect with people inside and outside of your community. You should always be networking. Even when you are at the gym or grocery store, you are networking. You must network as often as you can, even if you think you are too busy to do it. Your network is the equivalent to your net worth. Who you know can determine how far or high you intend to go.

Many people will network for the wrong reasons. Never network to just find a job or to sell your product or service. Some will go around passing out business cards while spilling drinks all over your shoes. They will add you to their mailing list and send you endless emails asking for your money. Some will go around begging for jobs just because they heard that certain people will be attending the events.

Other people network to escape their jobs or homes. They go to mingle and drink alcohol. Others will come to show off how popular they are or how successful they have been. If they are doing this, it is a clear sign that they are not who they say they are and it indicates that they are just living in pure vanity and ego.

When you do network, build meaningful relationships. Get in 2-5 meaningful conversations and follow up with who you meet. Make sure you take a break every hour for 10 minutes while networking. The last thing you want it to find that your makeup is running down your face or your mind is overwhelmed by hyper-saturating music, food, and conversation. If you have to eat, try to do it discreetly by walking away where no one is located. After you eat, return to the majority of people at the event. Do not come to a networking function or dinner for the sole purpose of eating. It is one of the most gluttonous things you can do.

Network at least once per month. Go to local service clubs or chamber events. Get with associations and designated networking groups. Build your contacts, even if you do not believe someone can help your cause. You may think that someone is irrelevant to your life or business now, but you never know who you will run into in the future or what you will need. They may need you too. Do not overlook the small things while networking.

Try to remember people's names and occupations and write them down on the appropriate business cards that you have collected from them. Be diligent enough to follow up with a phone call, email, or social media. As mentioned earlier, you network will largely determine your net worth. If you find that a particular networking group no longer benefits you or that you have outgrown it, simply move up to a better or bigger one. Networking will always promote you to have The Ultimate Advantage!

Be Healthy

You do not have to be a health fanatic, but being healthy in instrumental in who you are, what you do, how you do it. Have you ever seen a 50 year old who looks like they are in their 20's? What about a person who is in their 30's but looks like they are in their 50's? What you do to be healthy determines your quality of life. Some experts believe that is your own fault how your face and body looks after the age of 40.

Heredity can play a big role in your physical development, but much of the control goes back to you. Too many let their family's dispositions dictate their health. There is no reason why someone should be 100-200 pounds overweight. Neither should they be promoting diseases and cancer just because members of their family had it. Sadly, some people assume that they will have diabetes in the future. When they get it, they almost seem glad because they fit in with the family! Don't let this happen to you. Being healthy is a relatively easy thing to do. All you have to do is have the proper mindset. Being consistent is crucial too. Your inner thoughts affect your outer world.

A person who strives to be healthy must continuously train themselves in proper habits toward their lifestyle. They must know what food to eat and what exercises to do to give them the most results in life. Many people think that eating fruits and vegetables while waking up at 5 a.m. for a daily one mile jog is the salvation for healthy living. It is certainly a great idea, but there are many ways in which you can maneuver and create your own programs in which you will abide. You may elect to be or not to be as regimented as you like with your health programs.

Your program must work for you. If you cannot push celery and carrots down all day or keep a 6-pack, that is okay. It is not your obligation to do so. Magazines, television, and the internet will not determine your health, but you do. You can start by substituting it with your lunch for beginners. Eat the proper foods. Try not to overeat by watching your intake. It is best to eat according to the size of your clenched fist. Limit the amount of calories you eat. Beware of sweets and fatty foods. Evade the need for an overdose of salt. Run away from fast food and fried foods too. Not only will you gain weight, but it throws off your whole digestive system and forces you to be hungry sooner than you should be.

Drink 10 cups of water daily. Start with 2 cups a day if 10 seems too high. Try to substitute it with soft drinks and other non-water beverages. Avoid alcohol and cigarettes. Always have water available in every dwelling place. Drink 10-20 ounces before you go to sleep. It will renew your body and mind. Your body is a temple and it is the only place you have to live. Treat it as well as you want it to treat you.

You can also stay healthy by going for a regular fast. Fast by refraining from food completely for a whole day Do this 2-6 times per year to detox, lose weight, or gain discipline. If it is too challenging to go a whole day without food, just aim to miss a meal once in a while. This will easily shave a pound or more off of your body. Do not fast if you have a deficiency of some kind.

For exercising, exert your energy on something you love to do. Don't ever force yourself into a workout you do not believe in. Also, try not to compete with other people or do only what they are telling you. If you can't run 5 miles a day, just start at walking a half mile every day. You don't have to do what everyone seems to be doing. Exercise even when the time is inconvenient. Just find the right exercises that will suit your needs.

Strength, endurance, and cardio trainings are all essential for maximizing performance in life. Take up a favorite hobby like yoga, basketball, or weightlifting. Switch it up with swimming or rock-climbing. Just allocate an hour a day for exercise. Make sure you have fun when you are exercising too. Try to get a workout buddy, paid coach, or trainer to help you get the most out of your exercises.

When you find the right exercise and diet that fits your needs, you will be healthy for a long time. You will extend your life and increase your performance. You will look younger and fitter than ever. You don't have to be a model like the public media often promotes, but you do have to be able to get acquainted with certain physical requirements such as climbing the stairs to walking a parking lot (Assuming that you are able to walk and climb). If you find yourself constantly out of breath, get to the gym and cut out the bad food immediately. Being healthy can help you sleep less and allow you to work more. Having a healthy body and mind will give you a happy and sustainable lifestyle. Being healthy will give you leverage in your life and you will have The Ultimate Advantage!

Relationships

What is the purpose of living if you do not have great relationships in your life? Relationships are the gifts that you are given for being who you are. The quality and quantity of your relationships will be largely due to the quality of your thought life and self-esteem.

It is good to have 2 or 3 friends to call upon regularly. Check in with your friends and be available to them. Build your relationships by having a keep-in-touch method that works for you. You can visit people, send them emails, or make phone calls. You can also use social media and video chats to promote your friendships.

Friends are necessary because they complement us in ways in which we cannot help ourselves. Send your friends and acquaintances a "Thank You" card. Have you ever received a 'Thank You' card before? If you have, you know how good you feel when you get one with a personally inscribed note in it. There will be more about 'Thank You' cards later in this book.

Don't just keep friends for your own benefits. People know when you are trying to use them for your own benefits. On the contrary, there are certain people who will try to cling on to your life just because they know that you are resourceful. Stay away from these parasites. They will only drain you and move on to another target if you cannot provide what they have requested. They will even complain about you and invent rumors. Do not even bother with these kinds of people.

Invite your good friends to your events and keep them updated in what you are doing. Create relationships to the point where people remember you and reach out. When you focus on your relationships, you never know where they will take you. Sometimes you can make relationships in the strangest places and times. Relationships come up unexpectedly and a great friend in your life is hard to find.

Be sure to treat the people in your relationships the way you would like to be treated. Surprise them with a gift and give them a sincere hug and a kiss once in a while. Be able to take some time away from work and relax with those you trust. You can have friends for all sorts of reasons too. Sometimes you may have a running buddy who is not a good friend for the movies. Your intellectual mate may not be good for the football games. Keep spiritual friends of all different religions and gain great perspectives from all kinds of friends. You can always learn something new from everyone you meet. The right relationships will give you The Ultimate Advantage!

Coaching and Mentors

You need a coach or mentor if you want to be the best in what you do. It is good to have at least one coach or mentor, but it is more preferable to have 2-4 of them. You need them for different areas in your life. They can serve you in your spiritual, mental, physical, and intellectual capacity. You can also have a coach or a mentor for your hobbies to increase your performance.

Depending on what kind of coach or mentors you are looking for, you may have to pay. Some mentors or coaches demand a fee while others will do it for free. A good way around this is to try to do a favor for them. People respond quickly to favors. According to the Law of Reciprocity, people are more likely to do a favor for your when you do one for them. This is a good method to earn your way into a particular position with a coach or a mentor.

Coaches and mentors help you to develop the specific areas of your choice. They can also teach you about your profession or industry. You will learn how to model after their behavior as you study their characteristics and personality. They will propel you forward and cut months or even years off of the learning curve.

Hire a coach or mentor so that you can have an outside perspective. This person must have more experience than yourself. Communicate frequently with this person. The relationship with a coach or mentor can last for several days up to many years, depending on your needs. For a short-term relationship, you may hire a coach to help you with your golf swing for a day. For a long-term relationship, you would have a mentor or coach as your succeed them in their position at work after 20 years of learning the job of your predecessor.

The guidance of a coach or mentor can leverage your experience to a whole new level. They can help you break free of the habits and behaviors that you did not formerly see. Always be ready for constructive feedback. Some coaches are easy on you, while others can whip you into shape with a disciplined and no-games approach. Find one or many that fits into your personality to help you deliver the best results. A coach or mentor will give you The Ultimate Advantage!

Mastermind

A Mastermind is a group of people preferably 2-30 people who hold the same values as you do. You can either create a Mastermind or be in one yourself. The Mastermind must be harmonious and meet regularly to discuss actions. A typical Mastermind meets several times per year. Many will meet 4-12 times per year, but some can meet dozens of times in a particular way. The meetings can be face-to-face or virtual.

This powerful group will help you reach your goals even faster. Each member of the group will be distinctively different. They work together to achieve a common end. The United States of America was founded by a Mastermind of 56 delegates who came together with a plan to become an independent country from the British. An ideal Mastermind will have members who truly believe that the group is more important than themselves as an individual.

Nothing great can ever be accomplished without a Mastermind. Only the greatest establishments begin this way. Many companies, governments, service clubs, school boards, and management teams can be considered a Mastermind. It usually starts with a person who has vision. The person who has vision would normally find those who can agree and follow his or her vision. Each member must be skillful and complementary to each other.

The reason why you want to join or create a Mastermind is because it can fuel your ambition. You will be around dedicated people who have the similar passion to what you believe in. To learn more about how you can join a Mastermind, you can simply do a Google search. There are plenty of people who await your contribution. It will further your cause and strengthen your belief. Being in a Mastermind group will give you The Ultimate Advantage!

Confidants

Every person needs at least one friend that they can trust. A confidant is a person who you confide with. This is a person who you can share personal matters with. Since 2012, there are over 7 billion people in the world. There is definitely one who is specifically designed to suit your needs.

All humans have problems that must be discussed privately. The worst thing in the world is a person who goes out into public and shares his or her problem with everyone they encounter. This person does this because they have no one to speak with privately and feels the urge to disclose personal information wherever they go.

Another thing that you can do that may become detrimental is not disclosing yourself to anyone. There are many people who will not share themselves personally with others because they have been betrayed in the past or simply do not feel the need to disclose personal matters. This kind of person will certainly feel lonely all of the time. They may also start overthinking things as they bottle up their emotions. This also leads to the feeling of unworthiness, self-doubt, and discouragement.

There are many psychological reasons for having a confidant in which you can share your concerns .You need to be able to sit down at least once per week and discuss openly what is going on in your life with someone you trust. Let your thoughts out and share what you have witnessed in the past and what you see in the future.

When you open up to others, others will open up to you. If you tell someone a secret about yourself, someone will feel obligated to share a secret about their own life. This is a perfect example of the 'Law of Reciprocity'. When you share your mind with a confidant, they will also help you in your challenges by offering insights that you may not have considered before.

Be sure to keep a good friend in your life. Having two will be better. The person with three or more friends should never take it for granted. If you have more than one confidant, it would be best to let your other confidant know that there is someone else that you trust as well. You can tell different secrets to different friends, but be sure they know about each other, otherwise they will lose your trust, which will be many times more difficult to regain.

You do not always have to be a verbal conversation with your confidant. You can also write lengthy letters (5-20 pages) to your confidant. An email works just as well. If you can keep this person for your entire life, this will be good. If you find that this person is not growing as quickly as you are, it is time to let them go and search for another. Your confidant should help you reach your goals, not hold you back. Many people do not become their full selves due to the obligation of being lifelong friends with another person. A good example of this are childhood friends or college roommates. Share yourself with who you trust. They will always be able to tell you something that you may have never seen in yourself.

To test out your relationship with your confidant, ask this question "What is the quality of our relationship on a 1-10 scale (10 being the best)?" If the answer is less than a 10, ask "What can I do to help it become a 10?" When you ask this question with a trustworthy friend, you will start to serve them and build a stronger bond than ever before. Having a trustworthy friend or friends will give your life The Ultimate Advantage!

Be Proficient at Math

Numbers will be everywhere you go. When it is time to understand them, you better be prepared. If you get a bill at the restaurant for $60, can you calculate the tip if you were tipping 15%? What about when see a 30% sale for a pair of pants at $80? Can you multiply and count as quickly as you should? Math is a major factor in succeeding in life.

Every week, you should write out simple math problems as it pertains to adding, subtracting, multiplying, and dividing. You can create the problems at the beginning of the day and solve them at the end of the night. You can also get a high-school or college workbook to help you advance on your math.

Another technique is to have someone quiz you on random equations. Have a trustworthy friend or family member as you questions about math related problems. This should help you advance quickly due to your faster ability to think. This person does not have to be good at math; they just have to have the correct answer. You can also teach people how to do math. Teaching is one of the fastest ways of learning.

You can also punch relevant numbers in the calculator. If you multiply, add, subtract, and divide numbers relevant to your life, you will be astounded of how your imagination will start to work. Dealing with numbers can certainly expand your mind and help you think sharply. No one will be able to fool you due to your math ability. There is no such thing as a person who is bad at math! Practice your competency in mathematics because it will give you The Ultimate Advantage!

Get Some Sleep

While it is great to wake up early and stay up late, you also need to get enough sleep. Many researchers suggest that you can get by with 8 hours of sleep, but you are far different than the people they studied. There are many ways to approach sleep.

Sleep helps you to rebuild your mind and body. It also expands your imagination. In fact, when you have a dream, you must ask yourself what it means and try to remember it as clearly as you can. Write it down as soon as possible. Resting by sleeping restores you and gives a whole new vitality that you would not have if you were tired.

You can get enough sleep by taking regular naps. Depending on your needs, taking a nap is something you may want to do. For some, it is very easy. For others, it is challenging. If you find yourself thinking too much and cannot sleep, try to think of something more serene that will tranquilize you into a more restful state. Another good idea is to read a very deep book that is full of descriptive content. Heavy ideas and concepts will quickly sedate you soundly to sleep.

Study your sleeping habits and find what works best for you. To get some ideas, study up on REM sleep and Polyphasic sleep. There are many ways to approach sleep. One size does not fit all in this area. Experiment on your off-days of work to see how you can find the best sleeping schedule.

Take a day of the week to sleep in for 9 or 10 hours to fully recharge your batteries. Many people think that sleeping is a waste of time, but it is only a waste of time when you lay around in bed. If you can wake up quickly, then you are doing the right thing. If you are laying around for 30-60 minutes, you should try to force yourself to get up as quickly as possible.

Sleeping is a marvelous solution when you need a break. Sometimes work can become overwhelming, especially as you are working on a specific challenge. A quick nap can refresh you and give you the ideas and inspiration to help you fix the problem. Imagine that, sleeping can give you solutions to your problems!

Take your sleep seriously. Don't oversleep or under sleep. If you find yourself drifting on the highway, pull over and get some rest. Limit or prohibit your caffeine intake. Caffeine can easily throw off your sleeping habits.

Try to stay consistent. Do not try to wake up at 5 a.m. one day and 12 p.m. the next. If you want to learn how to wake up earlier, just set your clock 5-10 minutes back every day until you achieve the time you were aiming for. Set your own schedule. If you travel to different time zones, sleep on the plane and get adequate rest before you enter your events. Adjust yourself back to your schedule as best as you can. Getting the right sleep will give you The Ultimate Advantage!

Clothing

Your clothes speak for you. The way you dress dictates the way most people will respond to you. Having the right wardrobe will help you out in so many ways. Not only will you look good, but you will feel confident and there is a great chance of performing on a higher level.

Keep your clothes neat and clean. Organize them and make sure they are wrinkle-free. Dry clean your formal clothing and have an outfit for all occasions. You should dress well in everything you do. Sometimes people dress nicely to work, but they will slack off on their clothing at the gym. Never dress less than best when you go out.

Be diligent in your preparation of clothing. Prepare them the day before and coordinate the colors as best as you can. Wear accessories and jewelry, but do not over-accessorize. Use cologne or perfume, but do not overindulge in it because many people are sensitive to the scent you may be wearing.

Make sure you wear a style that works for you. Do not try to do what someone else is doing. If you try to be someone else, who will be you? Many people will try to wear hats, suspenders, and certain shoes only to find out that it is not their style. If you commit this fashion crime, you will pay the penalty of feeling awkward and embarrassed. You may also end up looking awkward too.

Invest in your clothing. Buy the highest quality garments and don't concern yourself over your budget. Here is a great example: 2 pairs of pants at $50 will last you longer than 4 pairs of pants for $25. For now, we are assuming that the $50 pair of pants are of higher quality. They may both add up to $100, but the better quality will look and feel better most of the time. Most likely, you will be able to keep the more durable clothing longer. In the long run, higher quality clothing is the best solution almost all of the time.

Hire a fashion consultant who can help you dress. You may also want to take a couple magazines that fit your style and read them. Use the internet and get several good books on getting dressed. You can simply study and interview successful and well-dressed people around you and see what works for them. Take bits and pieces from everyone you encounter. By the way, you will observe that most successful people are well-dressed.

Your style of clothing will instantly win over half of the people you meet if you do it right. You will become more likeable and people will respond better. Your clothing can set you apart from the people around you. It can help you blend in or stand out, depending on your personality. Be diligent with your wardrobe and take time to match certain clothing. Use your clothing in the right fashion (pun intended) as you discover The Ultimate Advantage!

Public Speaking

Learning how to speak in front of an audience is the one of the fastest and best ways to grow as a person. Despite it being one of the biggest fears known to humans, it is certainly achievable. When you learn how to speak in public, it will raise your confidence, self-esteem, and your ability to connect with others. It is one of the best ways to learn how to communicate one-on-one or to a group. It is surely my favorite way to improve as a person.

It will also teach you your own body language and the body language of others. You will have more emotional and intellectual control when you are amongst others. You will be able to think way before you even speak. Your presence will be felt when you begin to speak. Public speaking challenges all of your faculties, from the tip of your toes to the crown on your head. It teaches you how to use your voice and reach people right where they are at.

The best way to start public speaking is to join a Toastmasters group near you. Toastmasters consist of over 300,000 members worldwide. They are dedicated when it comes to helping people become more effective leaders and advanced communicators. They will teach you deliberate ways of getting your message across more tactfully. You can also speak to civic clubs or any informal meeting. There are always ways to find a way to practice your public speaking.

Learning how to speak in public will also help you learn how to tell stories. There is an old saying, "Facts tell, stories sell." This is very true. When you tell people a whole bunch of facts, they may be intrigued, but if you tell them a riveting and well-told emotional story, they will be more influenced by what you say.

You can also study other speakers by watching YouTube videos. TED Talks are an excellent example of this. If you watch a TED talk, you will see someone share their whole life story in a 15 minute segment. Learn how the professionals speak and then go out and try it for yourself. It is one of the greatest ways to test yourself and grow. Public Speaking will give you The Ultimate Advantage!

Have Something to Sell

Sales is the highest paying profession. If you are good at it, you can earn a lot of money. Everything is sold. The book you are reading, the pen you are using, the chair you are sitting on, and the car you are driving. Nothing in the world would exist without a sale taking place. You should always have a product or service to sell.

If you have something to sell, you will always have an income. Even if it is something small, at least you can earn something in addition to your full time work. With all the direct marketing companies like Amway, Mary Kay, energy companies, and many more, you can build your income to any level you truly desire. That's right! Selling products or services is the only way you can become a millionaire financially. Learning how to sell is a skill that anyone can learn.

That is the best thing about sales. You can become a independently wealthy within a decade if you find the right products or services that you believe in. You can even build an empire internationally based upon your products or services. If you are good at writing resumes, market it on the web and in-person by simply mentioning what you do. If you do 2 resumes per month for a fee, you are making a profit with virtually no expenses on your behalf.

What do you have that is valuable to others? Do you have books or movies? Are you good at landscaping? Can you handle cosmetics effectively? Can you instruct a lifeguard class part-time? You can even write your own book and publish it. You can sell your products and services and help thousands of people along the way. You can definitely deliver the results they need.

You can be very creative and come up with many ideas that can be valuable to others. People need what you **have**. You don't have to be the best at it; you just have to provide a good service. If you become so good at doing a certain endeavor, then you should consider starting a business. Starting a business isn't as hard as people say it is. You never know how far it can go.

Many people started out with a few homemade recipes only to find that they eventually became a multi-millionaire because of it. Use your talents and offer your goods and services to the public. You will be surprised with who will need you and how much you can help them. Finding products and services to sell will give you The Ultimate Advantage!

Build Vocabulary Everyday

You can always tell what kind of a person you are dealing with by the language that they choose to use. When you are listening to someone talk, you should be able to match their style and level of conversation. You should have more than enough words in your arsenal that you can easily slip them in to translate and paraphrase in your mind.

Reading the dictionary every day is a habit that the most successful people do. It may not seem like they do because they do not use big words, but it is certainly true because super successful people can navigate between different worlds of people, ideas, and places. They know the right words at the right times. It can all be credited to their careful study of vocabulary. When you can deliberately choose the right word, at the right time, for the right person, you will see how far you can go. Not only will your language guide you in conversation, but it will always drive you in your thinking and behavior.

Your mind will instantly become bigger when you can think of one thing in ten different ways. Poor and unsuccessful people can seldom come up with the right words at the right time. They stumble and mumble as they hesitatingly choose their words. Rich and successful leaders have an archive of words and their vocabularies can emotionally reach the minds as they range from the nadirs of the valleys to the apex of the mountains. Beware to never use $10 words where 5 cent words fit and vice-versa. Use the right words for the right person.

You can be speaking and thinking your way to success when you peruse the dictionary. Write the words you don't know, and pronounce them enough until your get it right. You should always be egregiously offended every time you meet a word you don't know, especially if you have seen it many times before. If you are not sure of a word while reading, make a note of it on a separate piece of paper and review the word later. Purchase a few different editions of vocabulary builders and dictionaries. Also, keep the Dictionary.com tab open every time you are on the computer. When your vocabulary becomes a force, you will have The Ultimate Advantage!

Learn How to Cook

This may seem like a strange suggestion, but learning how to cook is something every person should be able to do. There are millions of people in the world who do not know how to cook. They depend on others to make their meals. Some people reject to learn even the basics, such as cooking eggs or making cereals, although it isn't considered cooking by those who take the kitchen seriously.

Cooking will expand your creativity and allow you deep moments of thought. It will help you to concoct recipes that even you would not know you know. You can also impress your friends and family with cooking skills. You don't have to be an expert, but the basics can do you well.

Gain access to various recipes from cookbooks, TV, and the internet. Learn how to bake and prepare appetizers. Create your own beverages and grow your own fruits, vegetable, and meats if you can. Try to cook organic foods and use plenty of flavor while cooking in a healthy fashion.

Test yourself and your ability by trying a meal you have always wanted to make. If you ever fail, try it again another time. Become so good that you are unconsciously competent. This means that you will be able to produce a meal without even thinking about the steps that you take because you know it so well. You won't even look at your measurements and notice that you clean. Learn how to set the table correctly too. Throw on an apron and get into the kitchen. It will give you extra flavor to gain The Ultimate Advantage!

Don't Be a Slave Communication

Interruptions can instantly kill your day if you do not control it. They come about at all times of the day and must be dealt with immediately. Whether someone walks into your workspace, calls, texts, or send emails, you will have to know what to do in order to save your time.

The average American, will easily lose over 2 hours on communications that is completely unnecessary. With social media and other distractions on the internet, people are regularly a slave to communication. Some even treat it as a part-time job. You can lose a lot of time if your method of communication and finding pertinent information consumes you.

Anyone who tries to communicate with you has their own agenda. This is never a bad thing unless it completely takes you away from your goals as you cooperate with their communication sycophantically. Many people wake up and go to bed checking their emails and text messages. They are also eager to respond. This automatically puts you into a reactive state of mind instead of a proactive one. You are now waiting for people to tell you what to do rather than orchestrating your own life by creating your own demands for yourself.

Many people will become a slave to their communication so much that they will look down at their phones in the midst of a conversation. They will even glaze over the same emails and texts several times over. When a person walks into their office or workspace, they willingly chat the hour away instead of doing the work they know they should be doing.

To stop this, you have to focus on your goals and what you want to accomplish for the day. Allow yourself some extra time for miscellaneous activities and unexpected events during the day. It is best to allow 2 hours in your day that naturally go by. If you happened to keep your time, begin to work on tomorrow's tasks or even catch up on the old ones, but never allow yourself to give into any form of distractions just because you had a productive day up until that point. Give time for communication with others, but make most of it on your schedule. Don't let someone call your phone and take as long as they want. Limit your emails and texts as well. This takes up more time than many will think, even if you type fast. Learn how to say no to the extended minutes that could be yours.

When someone walks into your workspace, immediately get up and let them know that your full attention is on them. After you do this, ask "How can I help you?", "Is it something that can wait?" or "Would you mind talking about this later today?" Use whichever method you choose to let the person know that you are working. Of course, do not offend a person and always do it in love. When they acknowledge this, they will tell you what they need to tell you. If they have nothing to tell you, which happens most of the times, enjoy the extra time you have gained by practicing this discipline.

When you are working on a project, put away the phone and the emails. Keep all sights and sounds of any distractions away from you. Lock the door and get to work. If you can get long stretches of time to concentrate on your projects, you will get more of it done. When someone calls you and you cannot talk, simply let them know and call them back. You also do not have to answer ever phone call that rings, especially if you are not in the position to answer. Don't ever think that any of the tactics of defeating distractions are a form of being rude or disrespectful. In fact, you are rude and disrespectful to yourself if you let yourself become a slave to distracting communication.

Get your time back by learning your habits on communication. If you find that you are distracted for most of the day, it is probably due to your communication with others. It will surprise you how much time you will save when you take note of where you put your time in regards to communication and how you can change it for the better. Controlling your communication will help you gain The Ultimate Advantage!

Rules and Standards

Create a set of rules and standards for your own lifestyle. This will help you measure and manage what you do most of the time. This is basically a system that you establish for yourself to stay focused on your priorities. If there are anything that you do that you need reminded of, this will help you immensely. You can start out by writing them down on a piece of paper, stick tabs, corkboards, chalkboards, or your whiteboards.

You may set many rules for yourself. It is best to set your rules in monthly periods. For instance, you can make a rule to call your brother twice per month. You may have a rule to follow up with all people within 24 hours. Another rule could be to run 30 miles per month. You can read 2 books per month. You can have a rule to check emails every 6 or 8 hours. You can decide to wake up every day at 6 am, but sleep in one day out of the weekend. There are many rules that you can make for yourself. You can even include your hobbies such as photography, fishing, and nature walks.

Most people naturally do what they want to do anyways, but these rules and standards help you remember what may or may not be missing from your regularly scheduled life. Sometimes we forget what we truly enjoy due to certain reasons like seasons, finances, locations, other people, and so forth. Having standards and rules help you to remember what you love to do.

The standards and rules that you set for yourself keeps you of track and happy with life. When you start doing certain things subconsciously without your board, you can replace them with other habits. This is an excellent way to change your habits or keep them the same. Having standards and rules in your life will help you to gain The Ultimate Advantage!

Self-Talk

Talking to yourself is one of the most important things you can do. In a world where opinions float around, you have to protect your mind with your own positive affirmations. People can easily come by and tell you something that is not true about yourself. Sometimes, it may even be discouraging. Tell yourself how good you are and why you are happy to be here.

Make positive affirmations such as:
"I feel happy!"
"I feel healthy!"
"I feel terrific!"
"I like myself!"
"I am having a good day today!"

Talk yourself into great things. There are many people who tell themselves negative mindsets. When you ask them how they are feeling, they say, "Not bad, could be worse." What does that mean?!? Not bad as in not good? What could be worse according to this person? They say, "I feel sick" or "I can't complain." Are they that miserable that they give these weak assessments of their day?

Too many people start to drift along in life because they simply do not say the right things to themselves. They talk themselves out of jobs that they could take, places they can go, and even the kind of person they could be. The best way to solve this problem is to create a sheet of paper with positive affirmations. You can create your own and you can find more online.

Boldly state these positive affirmations every day as a habit and watch how quickly you soar in life. Repeat the affirmations every morning, midday, and night. When you do this, you will find yourself becoming more confident and you will start to do things you never knew your can do. Your eye contact will be penetrating and you will learn yourself better. There will be an extra pep in your step and you will be recognized by all you encounter. Your self-esteem will reach its highest point and you will feel unstoppable.

You will have a new vitality and discover new ways of thinking that you never had before. Your walking and talking will change. Everything around you will make a significant difference because "Every day in every way I am getting better and better!" Repeat these affirmations every day for the rest of your life. Positive affirmations will change your life and give you The Ultimate Advantage!

Attend Live Trainings

To advance your skills even further, you are going to want to attend a training program. When you go to a live training, it is far different than reading a book or watching a video. In fact, you get to interact and ask the trainer or speaker questions. This feeling of involvement gets your attention and helps you learn more about what is being taught.

There are different types of live trainings. There are webinars. This is a seminar on the web. There are plenty of them for almost every skillset that you can imagine. You can even host one yourself! There are workshops, which can be from two to several dozen people. They are typically longer than one hour. Seminars can be of any size with one or more teachers. Another training type are speeches, which are short and informative, entertaining, and inspiring. There are also panels and critiquing sessions that you can attend.

Whatever it is that you need, any type of training is available to you. You can attend a conference or convention and get it all. You can hear speeches, attend breakout sessions, and watch panelists debate deeply. The best part about attending live trainings is that you are able to get connected with other people who are there. You get to share information, ideas, stories, and you may even get a chance to make a friend and/or collaborate on a project.

A good rule of thumb would be to visit 2-4 live training sessions per year. It would be even better if you can go to one every month. When you go, take copious notes, ask tons of questions, and always sit in the front. Only the best students do these things. Make as many connections as you can and try to meet the teacher who is running the live training. Get involved in the training session and make the best of it. There are always teachers available for your to help advance your skills and help you find The Ultimate Advantage!

Have a 1st Class Mindset

Place yourself among the elite. Be around people who are smarter and wiser than you. Surround yourself with the best. You should always be in a room with people smarter than you. When you put yourself around the best people, you are more likely to become the best in everything you do. It is time for you to have a 1st Class Mindset.

Only the best people can help you excel in life. Not only do your people need to be the best, but also your resources. Get around the best neighborhoods. Go to the best libraries. Watch only the best movies. Eat only the best foods. Have only the best conversations. Send the best checks and stamps. If you are going to do any of these things, they might as well be the best you can find! This is what it means to have a 1st Class Mindset.

Too many people settle for less than best. They are often surprised when other people pass them in life. They think in inferior ways and expect inferior results. This happens because they have been taught to think inferiorly as people around them spoke highly of people who seemed superior have accrued a multitude of accolades. They feel that the best is unattainable because they are compared to others who have appeared to 'make it' in life. If you have a 1st Class Mindset, you will never settle for anything less than best. Upgrade every part of your life. You are just as good as the person who devours steak and wine on the romantic beaches (assuming that this is an ideal for some people).

If you are starting out and the best seems challenging at the moment, go and visit the best places you can find. You will most likely find the best people and the best resources. Visit the 5-star hotels, restaurants, and car dealerships. In fact, eat the best food on the menu and then go out and drive the best car you can find in the best part of town.

Having a 1st Class Mindset requires you to jettison all of the old ideas of yourself that you had before. When you look around, ask yourself, "Is this the best there is?" If it is not, go out and get the best that life has to offer.

There is no sense sitting in economy class in the airplane when the 1st Class seats are open and waiting for you. Take the best seat if it is available to you!

This mindset will lead you into prosperity and lead you into riches that you would have never imagined before. If you are going to be in this world, select only the best of the best. Let others get what they think they deserve while you experience 1st Class treatment. That is the only way you can teach others how to indulge in the 1st Class Mindset. There are 1st class ways to look at every area in your life, and when you do, you will experience The Ultimate Advantage!

Plan out Your Life

Anyone who has a plan in life will be able to attain almost all of their goals. Take a day out of your life and think about what you really want out of life. Sit down and plan it out with yourself or with whom you trust and intend to live your life with. This will stimulate you in the highest order and help you realize that everything you can possibly ask for is actually quite attainable.

Planning out your life requires deep thought. It is similar to a 'bucket list', except for the fact that you are not focusing on what you will do before you die but rather what you will do while you still have many years to live. When you have a solid plan and begin to work that plan, you will find that things and circumstances will start to align themselves according to your plan.

The reason why most people do not do this is because thinking and planning can become very belaboring. If you ask a man to talk about everything he ever wanted, he will deny his wants in the long-term because he is so focused on the short term. Thinking far ahead can really hurt those with transient perspectives, especially when they do not have a long-term and life-long plan. That is exactly why you should plan out your whole life.

Plan out the kind of children you want to have. The kind of marriage you want to have. Plan how you will retire. You can even create your own obituary and write out your accomplishments in your eulogy! Plan out how many countries you will travel to and the kinds of hobbies you will start to undertake. Just write them all out at first, then go back and edit when your creativity slows down.

If you need help with this, think about what you wanted ever since you were a child. Ask your parents and family members about the things they believe your are most passionate about. Talk to your spouse or best friends and ask them about if they are willing to go through certain experiences with you as you make your plans. Do not adjust your plans according to how you are now, but who you can become in the future. Plan 5, 10, 20, and 50 years down the line. Contact me personally

@ www.danielally.com. I can help you in this area. Your life plans will help you discover The Ultimate Advantage!

Become an Expert

In your chosen field of work, excellence is in demand. Your field has a opportunity for you to become your best personally and professionally. If not, then it is time to find another line of work. Your potential is waiting for you. If you do not like what you do, decide to develop yourself and flourish in other skillsets. Put your talents where it can be maximized by the work that you do. Make yourself into the best instrument you can be. In due time, you will surely be used. Everyone can use a good instrument.

When deciding to become an expert, choose something that you love. Make sure that it is your passion. If you are an artist of any kind, learn everything you can about it. If you are in a particular industry, read all of the latest news and details about where your industry is heading. Go to various trade shows and conventions. Study the best people around you. Success always leaves trails.

There are experts in every field. You might as well become one too. Read deeply into what you do and learn how to navigate in your world of work until your efforts become subconscious. When this starts to happen, go for more challenging work so that you can stretch yourself to your highest potential. An expert becomes an expert because he or she elects for further growth.

If you can practice your craft, do so. Learn to practice at any time of the day. Always be thinking about how you can become better at your work. Learn all of the nuances. You should be able to answer 90% of the reasonable questions that people ask you. If you cannot, you must strive to find the answer to the question that was being asked.

Becoming an expert is fun, but challenging. It requires you to put all of your life into your work. If you think about it, your work is one of the most fulfilling things that you can do. Try to put a spin into it and create innovative approaches. Become an expert to the point where you do not know how to quit. Do it so well that you forget how old you are. Let people know that you are an expert by marketing your talents.

Go crazy over the work that you do. Be able to casually slip in your expertise in every area of your life. Get lost in your work. Money will come according to the quantity and quality of service that you render, in accordance to your expertise. When you become an expert by studying, practicing, and applying your work, you will be very happy with your life and you will experience The Ultimate Advantage!

Invest in Yourself

Education will always be your best investment. Surprisingly, many people will value entertainment higher than education. The value you receive from entertainment is too ephemeral for the price you pay for it. Always put education in front of entertainment. It will last longer. Many people make the mistake of pouring their finances into meaningless activities such as entertainment. These expenditures do not help you in the long-term. They are usually forgotten the next week and cost a fortune. For instance, to take another person out to an amusement park could cost well over $100. This same $100 could be applied to 5-10 great personal development books or a content-packed seminar. Many people will not make education a priority. They think that education stops after high school or college.

    They may even go as far to consider their professional development classes too much of an investment. This is probably due to the fact that our educational system is laced with boredom since the very beginning of a student's formal education. Children would be so excited to participate in Kindergarten, but by the time they are seniors in high school, they no longer delight in learning because they feel obligated to regurgitate facts rather than learning relevant life skills. Remembering 101 reasons for the Civil War is not as interested as learning life skills such as marriage, finances, taxes, law, goals, and relationships. The great philosopher, Jim Rohn once said, "Formal education will make you a living, self-education will make you a fortune." The fortune seems more feasible.

Regardless of this great plight, you must be willing to deliberately pay the price of your learning materials. This means that you are constantly buying audios, Books, e-books, DVDs, seminars, college courses, and coaching sessions. This means that you are putting at least 10% of your income into learning more about yourself and your profession. Choose your specific area of growth and work on it for several weeks at a time.

Benjamin Franklin once said that "An investment in knowledge pays the best interest." Knowledge from real education has a long term effect. Even if your learned skill has become dormant, you can always resurrect it by practicing. It is like riding a bike. Do you really forget how to ride a bike? It may be hard at first if you haven't done it in years, but if you try to ride, you will probably relearn it once the day is done. It is the same with other skills you learn.

Please notice that it doesn't always cost money to invest in yourself. You can find many insights, wisdom, and worthy information from other sources. You can go to many free places such as the library, internet, and other people. Take the time and learn everything you want to learn. You become a better person overall when you take the time to learn.

If you decide to invest in yourself, the dividends in the future will flow. It will become self-evident. People will recognize that you are educated and you will not be exploited. Not only will you be richer financially in the long-term, but you will be healthier, stronger, better, smarter, and wiser. If you invest in yourself, you are really investing in your future. The purpose of living is growth. When you grow yourself and know yourself, you will be more fulfilled and happy as a person because you will make substantial contributions. Invest in yourself and you will obtain The Ultimate Advantage!

Listen to Audio Programs

Your commuting time can dramatically change when you take on the habit of listening to audio programs. Most Americans commute for an average of 10-15 hours or more per week. This means that if you can take the time to listen to informative lessons, you can gain the education of a full 4-year institution in less than 2 years!

When most people are driving, they are more likely to be in their subconscious mind due to experiencing an almost mindless task. You are more likely about to learn when you doing a light task, such as driving. Instead of listening to music or talk shows, you can be gaining access to more knowledge.

Your audio programs can be filled with speeches, discussions, audiobooks, interviews, and the like. You can get audio programs at your local library. You can download them or buy them from a particular source on the web or the stores. You can also use your smartphone or gadget.

Try to put to use everything that you learn in the audio programs. Your mind will be open to suggestions and when you use this powerful commute time to learn, you will be way ahead of the game. Be sure to pause the audio program to think about what is being said. Try to find a way to record your thoughts on a voice recorder as safely as you can.

Listening to audio programs will change your life. Whether you choose to learn one subject or multiple subjects, you will compile massive pieces of knowledge. Audio programs are great to listen to if you want to learn something outside of your profession. You can study fun things like religion, history, art, or anything that appeals to you. In fact, you can even create your own audio program and listen to it. Listening to audio programs will help you drive right into The Ultimate Advantage!

To-Do List

Some people keep to-do lists only for meetings, grocery shopping, and packing for vacations, but they often forget to take account for their daily tasks of the day. Each day brings a surfeit of surprises and we shall make room for them. Do you try to do too much in a day? Perhaps you may be doing 15-20 tasks per day when you should really be focusing on the top 2-4 per day. If you do too much in one day, you will let yourself down and your performance will not be consistent.

The attention will be diverted and will be weakened because of your inability to handle all at once. We must focus on one task at a time. Everyone knows this, but few people do it. As we hear people say, "He is a jack of all trade, and a master of none." This is not a compliment most of the time. It usually means that a person has various skills and is mediocre at all, but proficient at none.

Being a 'multi-tasker' is not good as well. You can't do two or three things at a time and be good at it. It is too unfortunate that 'multi-tasking' has become an acceptable theme. A person should be able to master at least one thing in their lifespan. Aim for mastery and you will be successful.

This is how you do it. In a typical 16 hour waking day, you can only get 2-4 major things done. Most people are ineffective because they minimize their strengths trying to please everyone and everything. They take the shotgun approach, which has no aim. It is unlikely that you can work out, garden, read, plan, think, watch television, cook, take your kids out, eat, and walk the dog in five hours in the most effective way. Some will even try to do little things to get momentum, only to find that they are tired before they begin their priorities.

You can probably do it, but you would be cheating the attention of your most important tasks. You won't be able to do all of them to the best of your ability. Do less, get more. Don't major on minors. Try not to 'multi-task'. Focus on what is really important. Keep a to-do list of 2-4 different items per day and knock it out as you build a system of accomplishment. These accomplishments will give you momentum like never before. Momentum is the name of the game. Once you start going, you will never look back. Create an avalanche of successes.

As you go through the list, cross off everything that you have accomplished. Keep the list with you at all times and work it thoroughly during the day. This will give you more strength and enthusiasm because your mind will be programmed to know that you are producing. Eventually, you will find yourself taking on bigger tasks after you are able to master the smaller ones. Let this technique give you The Ultimate Advantage!

Practice Pitch

Be able to explain who you are, because no one will do it for you. When you have a perfect pitch, you will be confident while you approach people. Your pitch will tell them who you are, what you represent, where you are going, and what you do in your life. It will make the perfect segue into natural-flowing and meaningful conversation.

Your pitch should be 15-30 seconds. It should explain who you are in that brief moment of time. You should also be able to shorten your approach to 5-7 seconds in case the encounter is faster than normal. Your pitch will help you with your first impression. You will be able to connect with more people. A pitch is a vocal business card that gets people to remember you. When they look at your actual business card, they will remember you by the words you said in your pitch.

Your pitch must be practiced hundreds of times. It must be well-timed too. Use the mirror and video camera to practice your pitch. When you get into real interaction with people, your timing is very crucial. You will hear people pitch at the wrong times all the time. There will be background noise or distractions that will not let them focus on what needs to be communicated. Make sure you have the full attention of the person you pitch to.

Be able to pitch in multiple ways too. One tone will not work well. Mix it up. Also add in multiple pitches. You pitch must be worked on for the rest of your life. The pitch is important to not only those you talk to, but yourself. If you find yourself pitching something that you are not passionate about, change the pitch. Make sure your pitch is always passionate.

The pitch you use should be so good and well-rehearsed that you can bring it up at the most unexpected times. You should be able to slip it in without force during any kind of conversation, as if it were your expertise. The three most important parts of your pitch is timing, accuracy, and passion. Be able to articulate all of the benefits that you have to contribute.

When you finish your pitch, people should know exactly what you do and how you may be able to help them. Be sure to customize your pitch, because everyone is different. Your pitch will help you gain The Ultimate Advantage!

Feed your Faith

We all need faith in everything we do. Without faith, nothing would ever get accomplished. Trusting in what you believe is essential in life. You must learn how to feed your faith so that your fears will starve to death. Faith is knowing that what you want will come to fruition, as long as you truly believe it. There are many ways that you can feed your faith.

You can read stories from fiction or non-fiction books. Understanding other people's stories can strengthen your faith. You can read religious texts, respective of your religion. You can go to a religious institute, such as a church. You can pray, which will help you gain access to your mind and help you rediscover what you already know.

Your faith must be taken seriously. If you lose faith, it will impact every area of your life. When you have faith, you will be an unstoppable force, hopefully the good kind. You will accomplish anything according to your faith. You faith will dictate your accomplishments and breakthroughs. A higher faith will give you a better life.

If you have faith in God, believe fully. If you have faith in people, believe all the way. Don't let anything discourage your from your faith. If you have a particular faith, study it, practice it, apply it, and teach it. Let your faith become contagious. Your faith should be worked upon every day. Things will be added unto you according to your faith.

Faith doesn't always have to be spiritual. You can have faith that you can persevere. You can have faith your this book will help you. Faith could be the name of a woman. You can have faith that the chair your are sitting on won't break. Whatever you do, have the kind of faith that you want and believe as deeply as your can. Doubt is the enemy of greatness. It is also the opposite of faith. Faith makes keeps you encouraged. Your faith will give you access to The Ultimate Advantage!

Use the Phone

If you are in business, you should know how important it is to use the phone. The phone will help you earn more friends and will increase your income when you choose to use it correctly. If you a salesperson, recruits, entrepreneur, or the like, you must commit to a certain amount of calls per week. The more calls you make, the more likely your business will develop.

A good rule of thumb is to make 25 calls per day. It would be even better if you made most of your calls before noon. Most business is done before the noon hours. People are more likely to take the afternoon slower than they would in the morning. If you can make 10 calls before 10 am, that would be even better. Be sure to set up your phone calls the night before so that you can start making business calls by 7-9 am, depending on your style.

If you make 25 calls per day, you can easily make 500 contacts per month. If you make 500 contacts per month, even as an inexperienced person, you can get at least 10% of the people to return your call and 1-5% of people to do business with you. That is the worst case scenario. Of course, it can become far better. You can do business with half of the people you call and you can eventually hire other people to make your calls. Referrals are also a great opportunity to grow your business. The possibilities are endless.

Making phone calls is one of the fastest ways you will be able to gain financial freedom. The fear of rejection should never stop you from making a call. There are people waiting for you to call. Your calls do not only have to be business focused. You can call family and friends and family too. Make sure you are strategic with your calls.

Also, follow up on all of your calls. Most people do not follow up. Create some kind of follow-up system that works best with your habits. Use a calendar to keep track of who you need to follow-up on. You can also keep a database. Always keep a pen and paper at hand too. You can be sure that you will have to write down what you learn.

Create a script for yourself to assist you in your calls. Whether you are sending emails or making calls, you want to address people by their names. Be as authentic as you can be. People like people who can sincerely relate to them. Of course, you would want to customize everything you write and say if you are using a script. Make sure you smile when you dial. People can sense certainty on the phone. They can also sense apprehension. Be sure to use verbal cues like laughter and audible agreements. To speak with more authority on the phone, stand up. Your physical shift will dramatically impact the way you speak on the phone.

Another key is to invest more time with better prospects. Better prospects will give you better answers. The way you find better prospects is to get the bad ones out the way first. Trial and error may be the key. Load your gun, cock it, aim, and fire away! Make as many calls as you can. Delete the bottom 20% of your business every 6-12 months.

Break through all of the noise in their mind when you call. Learn how to get past the gatekeepers to reach the decision-makers more quickly. Do not feel rejected what they use the phone. When you are on the phone, sell the appointment, not the product or service. Acknowledge the fact that most people have caller identification. Always leave a message on the other person's voicemail. It should not be more than 30 seconds. Never expect people to call you back either, even if they promise they will. Using the phone correctly will give you The Ultimate Advantage!

Create Videos

A good technique to help yourself and others is to create videos. Fewer people are reading books because the internet is providing thousands of videos every day. There are millions being produced every month. People are posting all kinds of videos for different reasons. If you wanted to learn a new recipe or how to do your make-up, you will find thousands of videos online.

There are just certain things that can be done in videos that other types of media cannot do. You have a skill or talent that you need to showcase that can be done via video. People can definitely learn from what you have to offer. There are people waiting for you to teach them what you know. People will leave comments and like your videos too. You will appreciate all the complements you get from your new fans. If people harass you online, don't pay attention. They are probably bored with life or may not understand where you are coming from.

If you are in business, this is an excellent marketing tool. People are always searching for new and better ways to accomplish more. Sometimes a still picture or words cannot do the job. Creating dynamic videos will get your talents across and help them understand your personality. People like people who like people. They are also more likely to buy from those they know, like, and trust. This is especially true when they feel like there is mutual understanding after they review your video.

Not only will you be able to help others with what you teach or entertain, but you will also work on your presentation skills simultaneously. The video world is almost like being on television. Everyone can be seen and heard. You can put on a performance if you want. If you catch something in your life randomly, you can post a video about it too. The videos do not only have to be about you, but it could be about what fascinates you. There have been thousands of videos that have gone viral and people have instantly become famous because of it. Although becoming famous might not be your goal, it can certainly help if you have something that other people want. Posting videos, whether it be for personal or professional reasons will give you The Ultimate Advantage!

Know Peoples Names

The sweetest sound to another person is their name. Calling someone by their name instantly boosts their confidence, your credibility, and mutual respect. You become far more likeable when you remember someone's name. It is even better when you meet someone in the future and remember their names, even if it was months or years since you have met them. It is also impressive when you learn to say and spell a challenging name.

Remembering names seem to be difficult, but it is actually easy. All you have to do is associate it with someone else that you know or a brand of food that you recognize. For instance, my secretary's name is 'Shivanee'. Most people do not even try to say her name because it seems so challenging. She has gotten dozens of false pronunciations because of her name. It is pronounced 'Shiv-ah-knee', but an easy way to remember it is by the Greek yogurt named 'Chobani'. Although it is not the same spelling, it sounds similar and it relates to what most people already know. She often feels that people care more if they learn how to spell and say her name.

You can also create your own mnemonics by creating an image in your mind when you first meet a person. If a person's name is Matt, you can picture him sitting on a big rug or mat with an apple on his head. It seems like a strange image, but the stranger it is, the easier it will be to remember his name. All you have to do is draw a picture in your mind when you first meet someone. You are more likely to remember their names.

Most people say, "I don't do well with names." This is just an excuse to not remember someone's name. They are basically saying, "I am going to forget your name because it is not important enough to remember." The quickest way to remember a person's name in a conversation is to say their name in your head a dozen times, then try to use it at least 3 times during the conversation you have with them. Be sure not to overuse their name, otherwise you will sound like a phony person.

When you walk into a room of 10 people, you should instantly learn their names and memorize them. This will give you power and help you get the attention that you need when you need it. There are so many cases where people in public wear name tags. When you say their names, their faces immediately brightens and they are more willing to comply. Many people are afraid to ask others for favors just because they don't remember their names.

You will begin to gain more friends when you remember their names. It is another way to display your affection for another person. Cycle through people's names as much as you can as you think of them, especially if you see them frequently. People will start to think highly of you and you will be favored by them just because you used this technique. You will also get a bigger bank account because remembering names will give you The Ultimate Advantage!

Smile as Often as Possible

One of the greatest ways to be tactful is to smile. People love genuine smiles. It is one of the most sincere forms of love. It also costs you nothing. A nice smile can brighten up your day. It can also change the dynamics of another person's day. Smiling is one of the best ways to show appreciation. Almost everyone has a nice smile and it should be used.

You can even smile when you talk on the telephone. People can almost feel your smile, even if they cannot see you. Smiling is a wonderful cue for non-verbal communication. It tells people that you are confident and easy to deal with. No one likes to deal with people who are difficult to deal with.

Beware of the fake smiles. Sometimes you may run into someone who just cursed another person out and will return to you with an insincere smile. Some people think that they can 'fake it until they make it'. However, it is easy to detect a fake smile. You can tell because only part of their face moves. A real smile includes your eyes. Yes, it is true, we smile with our eyes.

Sometimes you can smile yourself into happiness. If you ever get down, you can smile and you will begin to feel better. It is far easier to smile than it is to frown. One study shows that the face has 43 muscles and it takes 10-17 muscles to smile, while it takes 20-28 muscles to frown. It seems like you are far better off smiling. It seems to be far more beneficial.

Mother Teresa once said "Peace begins with a smile." Dr. Seuss also said, "Don't cry because it's over, smile because it happened." Smiling makes us happy. With little effort, you can change the face of the world (pun intended). Smiling will make your day and those around you better. Smiling will give you The Ultimate Advantage!

Observe People

Be curious about all the people around you. People will teach you many things about yourself and those around you. The ways that they act could very well be a good reflection of your personal attitude. If you sense dissatisfaction about your life overall or the people among you, it is not because of them, it is because of you.

What you see in others is most likely what they see in you. You have the opportunity to study those around you. From your observations, you can make a decision if you deliberately want to stay around the people you are with or if you want to move to a higher level. It is often challenging to become professional if you are around unprofessional people.

You can learn a lot from what you see in others. If you choose to see good things in people, you will get good results from them. If you see only bad things in people, you will most likely be upset with what you find.

Always expect the best out of others. They will also expect the best out of you.

People repeat bromides and platitudes all the time. If you find yourself in a flood of this conformity, realize that it is time to change. If you find that most of the people around you are mostly the same as they were 5 years ago, then you might be just the same as well. Switch it up by surrounding yourself with other people who are progressing in life.

If you want to be excited, surround yourself with exciting people. If you want to be bored, get with boring people. Not everyone will have the same vision of you. If you find that the people around you are not measuring up to your standards, it may be time for you to find a new environment. There are many people and places that can use your valuable presence.

Watch the mannerisms of the people around you. Understand body language and facial expressions. Body language and facial expressions can tell you a lot about the people in which you deal. Watch what people do with their hands and feet. As the old saying goes, "The feet are the honest part of the body." Study and learn why people yawn and sneeze. It isn't always because of the explanations most people tell you. See why certain people are tense, while others are laid back. Take up a course or read a book on body language and neuro-linguistics programming. It will give you deep knowledge into why certain people do what they do.

Understand why some speak fast, while others speak low. People walk and talk in certain ways. Most people are not deliberate in what they do during their days. They tend to drift along, waiting for something to change their days. Some people feel inferior to others while there are some who feel superior over others. Study why certain people quit and why others elect to stay. Seek to understand the motives. Motivation is the art of know why people do what they do. It is one of the greatest studies you can undertake.

There are many different personalities, cultures, backgrounds, mindsets, and creeds. Learn how to discern between the honest and dishonest. Help the needy and show concern. Some people require special attention from you when others could care less. Find out the differences and know the similarities. Everyone needs love, but we all need it to be expressed in different ways. We all have different love languages that must be dealt with accordingly.

Understand the minds and motives of those around you. Help others as long as it isn't an expense to your life. Some will ask of much and others will ask of little. Know your people. Be able to relate and connect. Give them what they want. The first place to start understanding people are the members in your family. What you see in others could be what you see in yourself. When you understand people by observing them, you will gain The Ultimate Advantage!

Learn How to Say 'No'

There are thousands of people who will come to solicit your help. Some of them are very legitimate offers, while others are only there to eradicate your time. There is nothing worse than wasting your time with something or someone you do not believe in. Many people waste precious time because they have not learned how to say 'No'.

For those who intend to take your time by using their own agenda, they will most likely put you in a guilt trap. They will make it seem that if you do not comply, you will not be considered a helpful person. They make it seem that you won't be considered part of the 'in-group' any longer. It will seem as if the entire community will leave you behind if you do not say 'yes'.

Saying 'yes' is how people are persuaded and how the sale is made. If people are consistently persuading and making sales on you, it's not their fault, but yours. If you don't want to keep feeling abused and misused, it is time to understand persuasion. A great book on this is called "Influence" by Robert Cialdini. The only way you will learn how to say 'No' is to understand why you would say 'Yes' in the first place.

People make concessions all the time to further their agenda. Some will not yield, even if you are not benefited. Millions of Americans take up weeks of time out of the year just because they do not know how to say no to offers. Some of the offers people say 'Yes' to should not even be considered in the first place, yet they know this, but do not take action on it. A good example of this is infomercials. People buy products when they watch an infomercial, even while they know these programs have taken their money before. They keep getting emotionally manipulated into buy things they do not need simply because they choose the quick fix.

Of course, if this happens to you, you cannot be upset with the person who allowed you to say 'Yes', because that would be you! Neither can you be upset with the methods and tactical approaches that were used or the people who have employed them. All you can do is learn what they do and what you can do on your part to stand your ground. Learning how to say 'No' at the right times will save you much time, money, and frustrations as you gain The Ultimate Advantage!

Hold Your Territory

Stand firmly on the ground and believe in who you are. Do not take unsolicited feedback or criticism. This is one of the quickest way for self-damnation. When an uninvited person comes by and tells you to change your style or approach, you will tempted to adapt to what they want, but if you do, you are likely to completely lose your own originality.

There are some people who will tell you to change because they cannot do what you do. They will tell you that it is only the 'outside perspective', but we all know it is not true. When strangers tell you to change something, especially when you know what you do works well, never consider their opinion.

Do not take all the advice you hear from strangers. Although some may be useful, most will only have you tippy-towing around who you actually are. Everyone loves to give advice and they will not be reluctant to share what they think about you, especially if you are open to hear it. There are many nitpickers, faultfinders, rule pushers, and charlatans who insist that their answer is the best answer. They will even throw a fit if you do not use it.

One time, a waitress insisted that I got her favorite shrimp recipe at a particular restaurant. Although I knew what I wanted, I did consider her offer. I didn't feel the mood to order what she suggested, so I didn't. Even though I went ahead with getting what I had originally craved for, instead of what she tried to order for me, she threw a major fit. She gave a plethora of excuses filled with details about why the decision I made was such a poor choice compared to what she wanted me to get. If I had gotten what she recommended, I would not have had the privilege of enjoying one of the best meals I ever had!

Many people will try to tell you how your work should be done. They will tell you want to eat and how to dress. They will order you around like you are a little child. They will tell you that you have to take a particular step before you take the step you want to get. They will tell you how to raise your family. Don't listen to these people. They are only naysayers who want to have influence. Do what makes sense to you. If you find that a suggestion doesn't work with your style, kindly express gratitude, but don't accept it.

The best way to get feedback is to ask someone you trust for constructive criticism. If you feel that there is something that you could be doing better and you need help, ask someone who knows how to help. Seek after those who can help you. Don't be criticized by someone you just met. Unsolicited feedback may seem feasible to adhere to, but most of it will put you in disarray.

Make sure you hold your territory. Be your own boss in your decisions. Don't get your haircut to please anyone. Get a haircut that you truly like. If you need and opinion, ask for it, but don't let people tell you what to do if they are not invited. There is an old saying that if you don't stand for anything, you will fall for everything. Be what you want to be, do what you want to do, go where you want to go. When you hold your territory, you will have The Ultimate Advantage!

Trust Yourself

Trust yourself in everything that you do. This may be cynical to some due to our imbalance and overabundance of flaws, but when it really comes down to it, we know the truth, and we should adhere to what we know.

In order to trust yourself, you must tell the truth to yourself all of the time. Trusting yourself is a matter of instinct. You are really trusting a Higher Power when you trust yourself. It is like a baby near the edge of the bed. The baby will reach the edge, but will seldom fall off because of divine guidance and protection.

Whether you trust yourself or God, trust your ability to make decisions. Trust that what you want will work in your favor as long as you do what it takes to get to a particular place. When you trust yourself with small things, added responsibilities will come to you. Trust yourself from morning until night. When you do, you will not be influenced by the subtle suggestions that are made thousands of times per day. Whether the suggestions come from external sources or internal sources, your conscious and subconscious mind should be able to guide you.

It will only be able to guide your ability to make clever decisions if you train it properly. If you know that you do not know something, try to find out enough information that you can trust yourself with it. If you know that you need to have more knowledge about a particular subject, do everything possible to obtain that knowledge until you and build enough trust with yourself.

When you trust yourself, you will tend to trust others. You will be able to know when someone is telling you the truth or a lie because you inherently know the truth. Only a liar thinks that everyone is a liar. Only an honest person thinks that everyone is honest. If you find yourself trusting people, that probably means that you trust yourself. It is a good test to find out how true you really are to yourself.

Trust yourself in everything you do. You have great powers within you that you have not discovered. You have talents, skills, and abilities that you have yet to use. You must realize that if you are decent at something, you can potentially be great at it. You will have to do some experimentation, but do realize that when you trust yourself, everything will work itself out. Your gifts will make room for you. Just make yourself an instrument, and you can be sure that someone will find use for you. This will only happen if you trust yourself. When you trust yourself, you will trust others, and this kind of trust will give you The Ultimate Advantage!

Take Responsibility

The difference between an immature person and a mature person is their duty of responsibility. When you take responsibility of your life, you learn much faster and you gain more power. The responsible person will know what is going on and how to deal with the challenges that life throws at them.

Even when it comes to the most infinitesimal and menial things, take responsibility. If you see a piece of trash on the street, go over and pick it up. If you see children fighting or arguing and you are the only one who can do anything about it, do it. If a pregnant woman needs your seat, get up. There are many opportunities that you will have to take responsibility. This is also how you demonstrate your power.

If you are big enough to take responsibility over as many things as you can, you will be put in charge. People will demand your leadership and expect you to deliver. The good thing about taking responsibility is that you have a chance to have dominion, assuming that you use it righteously.

The less responsibility you take, the less choices you have. Like the person who is on welfare, you will get only the minimal. You will be subjected into the hands of others and decisions will be made for you. There will be less joy, an empty bank account, more ignorance and false expectations on your behalf. People will not call on you because if you cannot handle yourself, you would not be able to handle them.

There are many blessings and virtues for those with a deep level of responsibility. They will have more respect from their peers, a highly-regarded reputation, and a larger bank account. They will receive joy and delight from those they serve and they will have more peace, wisdom, and understanding. In the end, the person who takes more responsibility over themselves and others will have a more abundant life and also experience fulfillment in everything they do. Taking responsibility will give you The Ultimate Advantage!

Leverage Everything

There are many things that can be done to leverage yourself. You can leverage your time, money, creativity, resources, and everything. When you use leverage, you are getting more out of what could be. You make the best of what you have and multiply yourself and your resources.

There are thousands of ways that you can leverage yourself in your life. You just have to look for the opportunities to do so. Instead of thinking of one particular way of doing something, there could be multiple ways. For instance, you can leverage your time by using paper plates and cups in your home when you are alone instead of washing your ceramics every day. This alone could save you one hour out of your day, even if it costs you $3. You must decide whether what you leverage is worth the cost of doing so.

You can leverage real estate. Instead of living in a 5 bedroom house by yourself, you can rent it out to someone else while you are living there as you live for free. You can leverage the people you hire by hiring one person instead of three. As you can tell, leveraging yourself is a simple way to be economical and savvy.

In traditional times, people would go out every evening to the store to buy bread and other foods. As they would go, they would take a long time doing so. By the time they got home they would be too tired to cook what they just bought because of the effort they put forth. A farmer would wake up early and milk all of the cows and neglect to hire someone to help, even when the help would make the most economic sense. People would often break their backs fetching water from the well or making plenty of trips in their horse and buggy.

Today, there are many people who take hours longer than they should by using old school methods instead using the simple faculty of thought. There are many ways one can dry clothes, but some would rather use the clothesline than the dryer. Just take a moment to realize what you could do to leverage your time to become more effective and efficient.

You don't have to be a robot, but you don't have to be a caveman either. Shaving cream works much better than any traditional methods. Instead of believing that you must put 12 hours of work into your day, maybe 6 would be good enough if you leverage yourself correctly. Your time, money, creativity, and resources have more value than you think. When you leverage yourself, you will have The Ultimate Advantage!

Never Take a Day Off (Except Sundays)

A real leader never takes a day off, except for Sundays. To be the most effective and produce the highest results, you must work 6 days straight with no break. If you really want to contribute the most, you should strive to work at least 12-16 hours per day. Don't worry about what other people say or think about your habits.

Of course, you will not work 16 hour days every day, but you will have an opportunity to do it a few times per week. You may begin to be tempted by offers to take time off with other people. You want to stay so focused that you forget that there is such an existence of a social life.

A social life really doesn't exist because if you are a real worker, you will always have the opportunity to socialize. There are always opportunities to run into people. When you do, make sure that it is mutually profitable. Do not delay your time or procrastinate. Always do it now!

They say that if a person in America works only 8 hours per day, they will only earn enough income to survive. For every hour after 8, you should thrive. If you only work 40-80 hours per week (including preparation and commute), you will always have discretionary time to do chores and work on yourself. Many great people work 6 or 7 days a week, 12-16 hours per day. They more you are serious about your work, they more you can help people. Be sure to work on your personal development too. Work on yourself harder than you do on your job.

This means that you should be exuding all of your efforts on learning and growing yourself and your work. If there is left over time, be sure to walk away from anything that leaves you thoughtless such as video game, television, or senseless internet browsing. If anything, save your resting time for Sunday or any other day of your choice. You will have plenty of time to rest then.

Force yourself to stay up and work as hard as you can in life. Live wholeheartedly and follow your dreams. Don't let anyone tell you that you are working too hard. Do not let their thoughts interfere with yours. Too many people waste their weekends, especially on Saturdays. They take hours doing everything that is non-work related. Don't let this happen to you.

If the people around you want to go to a cookout and drink beers for half of a day while gossiping or partaking in meaningless conversation, let them do it. Let them go out and watch a 4 hour baseball game or a 4 hour night at the movies. Let them take a day trip to the mall or spend the day at the pool. Stay home on that Saturday and read that entire book. It will be well worth the read! You can read a few dozens of books per year, just of you devoted your Saturdays as a reading day! As I said earlier, always put education in front of entertainment. It will last longer and pay off stupendously. Working everyday will give you The Ultimate Advantage!

Take Enormous Risks

If you ask senior citizens what they would change if they were to live their lives all over again, most of them would say that they would take more risks when they were younger. When it comes to success, you must take as many risks as you can. Take the biggest risk possible. You will either succeed the most or learn the fastest by failing. Fail as fast as possible so that you will know what to do next time. Regret is always worse than failure.

Taking big risks may not be the easiest thing for you and that is why you must start out with small risk. When you were a child, it was a risk to ride a bike, but when you learned it, you become very good at it. You probably started to do tricks too. It is the same with life and work. Our society pushes us to go toward security and teaches us to be risk-adverse, but this gives you no pay off or gratification.

If you take a risk, you will most likely yield higher results. Sometimes you may have to take a pay cut to start your own business. You may have to quit a job to attend a life-changing convention. You may have to drive 30 mph past the speed limit to get passed a drunk driver. Everything you do is a risk. You might as well take as many risks as you can.

The more you take risks, the more likely your risk-taking will become bigger. You may have to hit rock-bottom to reach up to the top. Not many people hit rock-bottom, and that is why they never reach the top. You must take a risk to win in life. Live a total regret-free life.

Most people will admit that they do not like to take risk, but if you ask someone who has experienced life, like the senior citizens mentioned earlier, you will hear them say, 'Take more risks'. You should take more risks just because no one else is doing it. Out of every one-hundred people, only five of them are really willing to take a risk to follow their dreams. It will give you more creativity than ever before. Sometimes risk is the safest route you can take. Sometimes risk is the only route you can take.

Since everything is risky, you might as well risk your life in everything you do. Is it really your life if you risk it to help others? The money and fulfillment goes to the person who is willing to experiment and risk more in life. Walt Disney would take his idea to 10 people and if all 10 people rejected it, he would immediately start working on his plans. Why? Because taking enormous risks will give you The Ultimate Advantage!

Be Flexible

You have to be flexible in everything that you do. It would be great if all of your ideals came to fruition, but it is unlikely true. When you are flexible with your plans, it will leave room for other things to enter into your life. Sometimes you may think that you want something specifically for you, but your Creator may not have seen it fit and because of your flexibility, you were able to adapt to your situation.

Inflexible people start to complain, compare, and compete. They start to look for all the wrong in the situation and tend to be sour about life. They practice their rigidity to the point where they break like a twig off of a tree. It is only the flexible people who can be wise enough to make the adjustment to prepare for something that is far better.

When you are flexible, it is easy to make decisions because you know what you want. You know what is the priority and you know that you will get it. Inflexible people are insecure because they are not sure if they will receive what they want, so they stare at a dead-end waiting for something to happen. When nothing happens, they bicker about it to other people who are staring at the wall with them.

Flexible people see opportunities, even if it does not align with what they had originally intended for. Sometimes life throws us curveballs to prepare us for the future. Sometimes things happen to us that makes no sense at the time, but we must be willing to look at the situation and ask ourselves, "What does this mean to me?"

When you realize that you cannot control everything, you will become more flexible in what you do. Flexibility is the key in dealing with people and circumstance. It takes a special type of tolerance to be able to deal with all kinds of people and get them to admire you. Flexibility allow you to be a chameleon for the moment in order to help yourself relate to the other person.

Be as flexible as you can with yourself, others, and circumstances. Be willing to accept the fact that things are divinely designed and orchestrated for your benefit. Being flexible will give you wisdom, insight, knowledge, and understanding. It will also give you tremendous room to grow. Flexibility is a major key to The Ultimate Advantage!

Celebrate

Be sure to take good care of yourself by celebrating properly. Take yourself out for your favorite meal or dessert. Go to the spa, take a warm bath, or watch a good movie. Go to the dealership and test drive an amazing car that you always wanted. Take a long vacation and indulge on yourself, especially after leading several productive weeks at work.

Celebrating properly is instrumental in your success because it gives you can incentive to work toward. Do not contradict yourself by working out extremely hard then rewarding yourself with a pizza pie or a half gallon of ice cream. This is not an act of celebration, this is an act of disorientation.

When you set up a celebration at the end that is reasonable, you will be willing to push much harder. It is one of the ways that most nine-to-fivers motivate themselves to work hard in their week, then relax on the weekend by whichever methods they choose.

Do something that makes you feel good. Don't work all week, punch-out, and then get intoxicated on Friday night only to be hung-over the weekend. Neither will you want to plop yourself on the couch for the night and snack the whole time. Find something that will push you for higher results, like taking a walk after a 2 hour stretch of work.

When you celebrate properly, you will enjoy your life because you have something to work toward. Make sure you enjoy your celebration with a friend or more. Be committed to celebrating for the right reasons and at the right times. Let your celebration be as great as your success as it motivates you to do more. Work hard and play harder. Celebrate in this good life, because it will give you The Ultimate Advantage!

Over-Communicate Your Message

Only the greatest leaders over-communicate their message. This means that they ensure that those around them understand what needs to be done. With repetition and clarity, you can be sure that those you over communicate with will get the message.

Over-communication is necessary because it is easy to get distracted in the business of living. When you over-communicate, you reinforce your message and its intensity. Also, just because you said something one way, people may learn it if you say it another way. Always apply the maxim: "Different strokes for different folks."

Some people like to be informed one way, while others prefer another way. Sometimes a person may have misheard your message. Not everyone has a laser-like focus. Some people get distracted, especially when there is more activity in this world than all time. People also play with their phones while receiving verbal messages. You may not see it as it occurs, but it happens all the time.

When you are faced with intelligent, more developed people, you may only need to communicate a message once. If you are dealing with a person of lower intelligence, you will want to communicate multiple times. Make sure you receive acknowledgement every time you communicate. If you do not, you will not always know if your message was accepted.

You will always need to communicate in different ways. For instance, body positioning, facial expressions, tone of voice, body and hand gestures may all apply. You can even use different channels such as social media, texting, email, phone call, video conferencing, memos, and any other source of communication. The only reason why you want to over-communicate is because everyone around you will always get the message. Deliver with clarity and repetition and people will understand. Over-communicating will give you The Ultimate Advantage!

Give Yourself Away

Always give without remembering; Receive without forgetting. Give from your heart, with no expectations to whom you give. When you give of yourself, you will be multiplied. Those to whom you give to will appreciate it, whether they know how to express their gratitude or not. Blessed is the giver who gives from the heart.

The liberal and cheerful giver is only planting seeds. They do not care whether they get back anything or not. They do not give to get. They give because they understand the Law of Sowing and Reaping. What you give can be multiplied thousands of times over.

There is a misconception that you must only give monetarily. This is not true. Money is not the only way you can give. People also place limits of what they should give. They say that a good standard of measure is 10% of what you earn. Although it is a good measure, you do not have to give 10%. You can give far more if you would like. You can give in time, ideas, counsel, gifts, or in any other way. There are so many people who need more from you than you money.

It is also important to give discreetly. There are many people who expect the trumpets to blast when they give. They want people to honor them by bowing down to them and placing flower petals where they walk. They want you to roll out the red carpet and treat them like a celebrity. These people will only receive recognition, but their lives will be completely empty.

The person who gives while expecting is like a person working at a fast-food restaurant expecting 5 cents for every burger he flips. Wanting something in return is not a good reason to give. You must give because your heart calls you to give. Do not expect to improve your reputation or status due to your level of giving.

There are certain people, particularly fathers, who think that buying their children toys are enough. They think taking them out once a month is good enough. They fail to acknowledge that just an hour of time each day is good enough for their child. Children want much more than money. They want time and love. Give your family what they need. Being the breadwinner is not good enough.

If you are going to give, make sure it is wholehearted. Give everything you have. Don't be concerned about getting it back. The way you give will determine the amount of satisfaction that you will receive overall. The secret of living is giving. The right kind of giving will give you The Ultimate Advantage!

Be Passionate

When it comes to living, be as passionate as you can be. There are too many opportunities to not be doing what you love. You must be passionate in your life. There are many people conducting lives of quiet desperation. There are also many people who work only to earn money, but deep inside, they despise what they do for a living. You can notice this great fact as you witness people grumble about their jobs in every part of the world.

Being passionate is easy when you find what you love. Many people will not take up the arts because they do not believe it pays financially, so they neglect it altogether. They will not become a musician or sculptor. People who have the potential to be great communicators will not put in the work to teach what they know because they know it doesn't pay the bills at first. There are so many people relinquishing their dreams just because they want a steady paycheck, company benefits, and two weeks of vacation.

Of course, there is more to life than money. Money is the byproduct of the service that you render. Doing a job only that you hate leads to jealousy, greed, hate, anger, envy, and will destroy your soul. When you are not doing what you are divinely designed to do, you may turn bitter within several months or years, even if it puts good money in your wallet.

Do not feel subjected the authority of your boss or circumstance. Understand that you have a choice to find meaning in your work and your life. If you doing believe in a certain thing, completely drop it. At one point of my life, I found that I was in three groups in which I was involved that I did not feel comfortable being with. I dropped all three one day and quickly found a dozen more that I could contribute to within a matter of weeks. No one from the three groups called me. They probably didn't like the groups either.

Living an unfulfilling life doesn't make sense, even if it pays the bills. There is no reason to be bored. You must find pleasure in your work. Go out and do something you love. Be passionate in your daily affairs.

Make small changes every day until your whole life involves full passion. Living a passion filled life will give you The Ultimate Advantage!

Reflect Daily

Every day, you will need a moment to reflect. Find a quiet place and cancel out all the noise. Select a comfortable place to think. Put away all technology and distractions. Force yourself to take a moment of 10-30 minutes each day to think. It will be better if you found an open or scenic view. You can even take a slow walk and reflect on your life. Reflecting is the greatest way to learn about yourself. You will receive insight, wisdom and understanding after you do it.

You will have a great chance to learn about your past when you take a moment to reflect. Think about your entire day before it is done. First, ask yourself, "What did I do right today?" Then ask yourself, "What would I change if I had to change anything about today?" Find solutions to your concerns and think about what you can do differently to have a better day tomorrow.

Reflect on potential opportunities in yourself. Count your blessings and give thanks for your friends. Think about what you can do to save more time. Write some of your ideas down. Figure out how you can take a more strategic approach. Changing your approach can help you out in many ways. Sometimes the new technique you come up due to your moments of reflection can revolutionize your life.

Take these moments of reflection in your journal too. Write new entries and review the past experiences. When you reflect, you will disallow yourself from making the same mistakes you have made in the past. If you are making the same mistakes and not changing anything, it is time to reflect. True reflection gives you wisdom. Wisdom is knowing what decisions to make and making it at the right time.

Think about how you can help the relationships in your life. Reflect on your early days. Learn what drives you from days of you childhood. Think about the future too. Visualize yourself doing great things. The more details you use, the better it will be. If your vision comes to fruition, it is because you have visualized it in the past because of your reflection time.

The time of reflection will help you breakthrough in life as it allows you to consider dropping certain patterns in your life. It will help you be more proactive and teach you how to respond to people and situations. When you take the time to reflect, it will pay off in dividends. Reflecting will give you The Ultimate Advantage!

Make Personal Sacrifices

Sometimes you will have to give up certain privileges for the benefit of something greater. Do not feel guilty about having to give something up. You may have to sell your luxury car to start a new business. You might have to give up fried food to lose 10 pounds or more. You may have to sleep earlier to wake up earlier. Make whatever sacrifices you need to make. Never let the good get in the way of the best.

Many people hesitate to make sacrifices due to their pride. They figure that if they sell their car in order to build their business, they won't be the 'guy with the Benz'. Some people will not quit school to start a business because they want to please their parents. A person may not be able to give up their season tickets to the ball game, instead of purchasing a seminar that would change their lives.

A personal sacrifice is not easy to make because there is much uncertainty. You do not know what to expect when you do it. When it's time to make a personal sacrifice, your emotions are at stake. The need for security kicks in and you may not know what to do. They want to be comfortable as well. They do not want to give up their security.

In order to get to the next level, you must be willing to give something up most of the time. This is why most people never reach higher levels. They are not willing to give the extra 10 or 20 hours a week of their 'video game' or television time to get a bigger promotion at work. They think that the short-term effects of playing the video game or watching television will yield them a higher reward. It only keeps you from obtaining the best.

Making personal sacrifices of your possession and time may be the move you need to make to attain a higher level. If the personal sacrifice seems relevant to what you are trying to earn, then go for it. Sometimes you have to give something good to get something better. Making the right personal sacrifices will give you the Ultimate Advantage.

Do the Right Thing

Your honesty will always be tested. Every single day you will choose to either develop or neglect your character. You will have the chance to embrace the truth or tell a lie. Doing the right thing requires deep examination of yourself. It calls for inspection of your heart. When it comes to witnessing a situation, you may be tempted to be dishonest due to your bias, but is it really worth it? If someone gives you extra change in a transaction, do you return it? Are you willing to tell the truth, even if it will be at your loss and your enemy's gain?

These are tough questions, but they call for the highest standards of ethics. People know who they can trust when they see who you are. Let your character speak for yourself. Your reputation is your best advertisement. Even a slice of dishonesty can throw away all of the years of hard work that you have completed.

In sports, there are certain athletes that cheat and others who play more than fairly. The person who knew he was barely out-of-bounds may be tempted to say that he wasn't just to preserve the win. There are only a few honest players who would be likely to admit that they really was out-of-bounds. These honest people are respected by their fans, coaches, teammates, friends, family, and mostly, themselves. It is the opposite for the villains who are dishonest. Some people cheat all the time. They cheat the whole game. They do whatever it takes, even if they have to trip another athlete just because the other person is running faster.

In business, an honest person can build his character, but it may cost him $250,000. Would he still be willing to do it? He just might, but it will hurt him to know that his competitor would not be as honest as him. It is true the short-term loss may be devastating, but there is plenty of long-term gain. His competitor may not be in business 10 years down the line, but his business may flourish due to the trust and respect that he has received from his clients. It is always worth doing the right thing.

Doing the right thing is the most respectful way of living. Even if you have to stand up to let an elderly woman sit down, it is worth it. Never sacrifice your values just because no one is looking. Don't think because other people are exploiting opportunities and taking advantage that you should too. You will witness many liars, cheaters, and thieves, but you must never partake in its evils.

These deceivers may win a false prize now, but they will not be around later. Their punishment awaits them as they dissipate in the future. The steady and honest person will always make it in the long run. Character is doing what is right, no matter what it is or when no one is looking. Developing the righteous and honest mindset will give you The Ultimate Advantage!

Take a Break

We often go through long periods of work without taking a break. It is easy to have pent-up frustrations due to the way life operates. A proper break will heal you and help you in everything you do. This is important as you put most of your life into your work. You just might need a break.

It seems feasible to take a three-day weekend off once a month. Take a 7-10 day vacation every 6 months. Take a month off every year. After 10 years, take a sabbatical to redefine your life and learn more about yourself. Taking time off will help you to manage your life and all of your affairs.

Always be seeking creative experiences. It is one way to expand your rapidly developing mind. Enjoy everything around you. Your environment contains many areas of influence. You can go from all ends to the spectrum such as nature to the fine arts. You have the ability to create your own experiences. Too many people do the typical things, but you can create your own. Go to a museum or stop at a park bench as you watch the traffic roar down the street. Watch a live performance or enjoy the chirping of the birds. There are many things to do.

You can even do a 'stay-cation'. This is where you choose to stay home if you travel a lot. You may have a deck, patio, terrace, or balcony that you can resort to. You can also catch up on reading or any of the hobbies that you miss. You may want to learn how to cook or even watch a few movies. There is always that chance to take time with your family. Clean up the house and try on some new outfits. Whatever you like to do at home, do it.

A spiritual retreat might also help. Take a weeklong spiritual examination. Go on a long walk or take a couple days by the ocean. Read your Scriptures and other religious texts. You can even get in touch with other groups as well. You may even want to fast for a couple days. Go to your designated place of worship and tranquility if you have one. Do whatever it takes to get in touch with your spiritual self.

Take a break to get in shape. Many people take a few months to drop massive pounds. Others will bike across Europe. You may want to develop the strongest muscles you can. Perhaps you may want to train for a marathon. Hike through one of the nature trails or go rock climbing. You might have a physical goal and a two week break or more can give you the time to accomplish it, depending on what you have in mind.

As you can see, there are many ways to take a break. Sometimes you need to step away to build your creativity. Taking a break will give you that time and everything to rebuild your soul, mind, emotions, and body. The break you take will give you The Ultimate Advantage!

Listen

Opening your ears is the best way you can open up your mind. Listening is essential in your lives. You must be able to listen to yourselves and listen to others as well. Listening helps us understand our present situation. You understand why certain things work the way they do by listening. You learn the most by listening to what people say. You can hear your own thoughts as people speak to you. Listening with your eyes are they most effective way of understanding another person.

When you listen to them, you can ascertain what they are thinking in their minds and also what they may be thinking about you too. You will find that the more you listen, the more people will appreciate you. God made two ears and one mouth for a reason and that reason is most likely so you can listen more than you speak.

Listening could be a struggle at first, but once you understand how it works, it will become much easier. It takes great efforts to become a better listener because there is so much that you naturally filter out. Most people like to give advice, opinions, and facts because they are always excited about what they have learned recently, but you may not listen because it is not what you are looking for.

As previously mentioned, the best way to listen is not with your ears, but with your eyes. When you have your eyes fixed on those you are communicating with (assuming you are communicating face-to-face), you will be able to show them the care that you actually have for them. People do not care about how much you know, but they just want to know how much you care. Lending your ears and eyes with full attention is one of the greatest gifts you can give anyone. Everyone enjoys a good listener.

Every person wants to feel important. When you listen, you make the other person feel like the most important person in the world. Always find something to be interested in. When you hear a key idea, story, expression, joke, or anything of the nature, formulate a kind complement and show the person your appreciation.

Paraphrase when necessary. If someone takes five minutes to say something, use just a few sentences to define what they just said. Nod your head and show that your attention is focused on them. Do not look elsewhere such as over their shoulder or to another person. This is a very insensitive and inconsiderate move.

Do not try to finish off the words of another person. Even if better word comes to your mind, let them finish. They will give you a sign for help at the right time after a long pause, sigh, hesitation, or deep frustration. This is where you smile and give them your gentle word or idea. Remember, timing is everything.

To take your listening to an advanced level, use a small book to start writing down the suggestions that people give you, even if you do not intend to use them immediately. You never know when they will come in handy. You can also repeat everything they are saying in your mind. This is a fashionable way to listen to others and show that you truly care about them.

Do not try to create your response when someone else is talking. People can see you thinking. Make sure that your responses show that you are listening. Try to also find out what people aren't saying by asking questions. Sometimes the things people aren't saying are far more important than the things they are saying. Questioning people shows that you are listening. It will also help you draw out more information and interpret what you heard in a much better way.

Truly effective listening will separate you from the pack. Listen openly with a kind heart. Try to remember something precious about a person. Do not be surprised if people tell you more than you deserve to hear. My previous book, "You Are the Boss!" covers the topic of listening more extensively. Listening will be your key to obtaining The Ultimate Advantage!

Thank You Cards

Have you ever received a 'Thank You' card before? Didn't it feel so special? There are very few people who write 'Thank You' cards. Try it by writing a handwritten note on a small postcard. Send it to someone you appreciate. You will be surprised by the response.

In today's world, we expect people to express gratitude in all ways except by a 'Thank You' card. What's even more important is that it is handwritten with a personal message inscribed within it. Many of the American president wives have written 'Thank You' cards for all kinds of people. No wonder their husbands have become so successful.

Not only do you give a different response, but you get a different response as well. Our world have lost the personal feel on staying in touch. Sending a 'Thank You' card is a warming way to say 'hello' as well. You can always write one to family and friends. You never need a special occasion to write one. In fact, it is better if you do not wait for special holidays or ceremonies.

Trying writing a 'Thank You' card today. Try to send one out once per month. Of course, you don't have to keep count, but the more you send out, the better it feels. The person who you send it to can also make a game out of it by sending you something bigger, like a basket-full of roses. This is where you step it up and get them a collection of their favorite books or an antique gift they have always wanted. Always out- give the giver. Distributing 'Thank You' cards will give you The Ultimate Advantage!

Express Gratitude

One of the greatest ways to obtain more in life is to appreciate what you already have. You have to take what you get, to get what you want out of life. Count your blessings each day and know what you are thankful for. At the end of each night, write down three things you are thankful for. They will be one of the greatest favors you can ever do for yourself.

Many people take life for granted and do not even realize that it is a gift to be a healthy, fully-functioning human being! We drive nice cars and eat good food. We must be thankful for the great pleasures that we have in our lives. Give praise and be thankful to its source. Think of how it was made and by whom it was made by. Cherish the moment as you were given a product or service that was done in a joyful manner. When you do such an act, you will begin to see the quality and quantity of what you have multiply. Not only will you get more, but you will have more to give because your 'cup runneth over'.

People begin to appreciate what they have when they are on the verge of losing it. That is not the way it should be. You have to consider it a blessing that you have it now. The more you have, the more you should be thankful. Stay mindful of how much you worked for it and know that there are many people who do not have the same privilege as you do.

You can also express gratitude to your loved ones. If you have a spouse, write down one attribute you appreciate about them each day. Keep this list with you and express them during romantic periods. If you ever get into a disagreement, bring this list out to quickly disarm the battle. Try it and watch how quickly you embrace your loved one.

Keep notice of the things you have. Recognize its source and its beginnings. Know that it will not last forever. Write down what you love about your life and count your blessings every day. When you express gratitude in what you have, you will never fall into the trap of complaining or condemning. You can always gain more and have it abundantly. Expressing gratitude will give you The Ultimate Advantage!

The Sexual Emotion

Using your sex emotion will be one of the biggest challenges for most people. It is the second most motivational emotion (Love is the first) and drives people to do crazy things. People will spend countless hours looking for an avenue to express their sexual emotions. You can actually use your sexual emotions to do something more powerful, instead of searching for an outlet of sexual release. Nevertheless, your sexual emotion must be expressed. Choose to express it righteously.

This may be a strange topic for you, but it is one of the most essential and least understood. Your sex emotion has the creative powers to stimulate your imagination on the highest level. Many people will misuse this power as they resort to thoughtless avenues such as pornography, strip clubs, and prostitutes. They may also partake in sexual behaviors with those whom they share no love with or even those of the same sex. The sex drive is so powerful that it can cause people to do diabolical things. People will get nefariously desperate to involve themselves in necrophilia, cannibalism, and bestiality.

The sex emotion is like an flowing stream that cannot be dammed up. If dammed, the stream will eventually overflow the dam and cause a disturbance to one's heart, soul, and mind. If this stream is contained by offering different methods of expression, you will retain your power and even gain more. The stream must flow and find a means of expression in order for your to reach more fulfilment and joy.

There is much more to learn about this amazing power of the sex emotion, but it will not be covered here. However, find out what triggers your sexual nature and find a way to transmute this overbearing sexual urge. Many times, words or pictures will trigger you and send a stimulating response to your mind and body.

When you control your mind, you can control your sexual habit. You will have control over one of the strongest emotions and you will be able to direct it toward something more meaningful in your life.

Expression of the sex emotion, if transmuted correctly, will help you to gain more power and discipline as you recognize it as being one of the major key factors for The Ultimate Advantage!

Relationships

Make all relationships right. Make sure you build strong relationships by calling on your friends and family members. Always keep it refreshed by sprinkling love in the mix. Reach out to new people that you meet and follow up. The best way to get friends is to be a friend yourself. You do not earn friends until you become one yourself.

When you become a friend, people want to be your friend. Give liberally and share your resources. Do not think that relationships will automatically work themselves out. They only work if you make a constant effort to improve them. Sometimes you have to remind people that you are still their friend or family member. When someone enters into your mind in the form of thought, call them as soon as you can. It usually means that they were thinking of your too. This is a great way to be a friend.

Also send gifts to your friends. Be sure to send them something that they like instead of a gift card, unless it is a store you know they like. Send them something personal, like a letter or poem. Show your appreciation for your friends. Let them know that you still exist and that you enjoy their companionship. Schedule a time to meet within the next three months.

On the opposite end of the spectrum, you may have to burn some bridges too. Sometimes you have to let go of certain people of your life. Delete them out of your life by leaving no trace behind. There are two types of friends: Those who pull you up and those who pull you down. If people are pulling you down, it is time to make the effort in finding someone who can replace them. If people are depleting your time, energy, money, and reputation, it is time to release them from your life. There is no sense in keeping a burden in your life. Don't depart by telling them off or any other execrable methods. Just let the relationship go as naturally as leaves fall from a tree. If you do have to tell them, be sure to be as kind as possible in your approach.

When you have a friend where you share mutual benefits, keep them. If you have a best friend who helps you, keep them too. Sometimes best friends change. Don't label someone your best friend for the rest of your life when someone else has been a better friend. That is the beginning of self-delusion. Make sure your friends are your friends too. There is nothing worse than a person who calls you their friend, but doesn't do anything about the relationship. Many acquaintances do this. Know the difference between a friend and an acquaintance.

An acquaintance is the person you may work with, a neighbor, or someone you see around town, but do not necessarily want to build a strong relationship with. However, there are certain acquaintances that you will want to have conversations with. Always be friendly, even if someone you know rubs you the wrong way. Also, turn acquaintances into friends if necessary.

For your family, you must be on top of certain relationships. Call you intermediate family often if you get along with them. If you have negative relative (who doesn't), don't let them convince you that you owe them something when you take off. Keep your distance from the scorpions and snakes in your family. Be prepared to never see certain people in your family again. Cut them off mercilessly if they are parasites in your life. Don't feel obligated to show up at weddings and funerals if you know in your heart that you should not go.

Overall, relationships must be monitored as carefully as a pageant applies cosmetics. They must be nurtured and developed. Keep control of who you are in contact with. Keep a list of people who you care about and who cares about you. Pray for them and call them when you feel necessary. You learn, earn, and return the average of the 5 people you invest the most time with. Your relationships will be one of the most ongoing decisions you will have to make. Also, don't forget to call your mother! Call your father! Call the people who raised you. Having the right relationships in your life will give you The Ultimate Advantage!

Your Most Influential Times

Every morning and night, an effort must be made to give your life for the sake of others. This decision begins from the plans that you made the night before, to the rest overnight, to when you first wake up in the morning. How do you prepare yourself when you wake up in the morning? What do you think about right before you sleep at night or when you awake in the morning?

The first and last 20 minutes of your day is the time in which you must influence yourself the most. You must decide what you want to do in the first and last part of your day. You may even switch it up, but you must stick to what you want you want to train and prepare your mind each day.

You can start and end your day with prayer, goal-setting, reading, yoga, exercise, light meals, thinking, writing, meditation, skill practice, visualization, stretching, positive affirmations, or anything productive. What you do in this time is crucial because it becomes the fuel that will set your day in full momentum. It will determine how you feel and how you interact with others.

Be sure to avoid toxins like alcohol, nicotine, emails, phone calls, or any kind of noise that distracts you from knowing yourself better. There are many reasons to take your day seriously. Give yourself the right fuel to get your engine roaring. Don't let traffic get in your way, but glide smoothly along the highway by beating the traffic with these maneuvers of preparation. Your morning and night habits will determine how will advance in this life. Awaking in the morning and retiring at night are your most influential times. When you use it correctly, you will have The Ultimate Advantage!

Have a Role Model(s)

Everyone needs a role model. Someone to look up to. We usually become like the people that we admire. If you find someone that is competent, confident, and courageous, you will most likely carry with you some of the characteristics of who you admire. We tend to become the people we study and appreciate.

Be sure to acknowledge someone you admire, but don't try to be exactly like them. Take what they have and be like yourself. If you try to be like someone else, then who will be you? Your role model doesn't even have to look like you. They do not even have to be in the same profession. You can still admire your role model(s) because of who they are and what they represent. You may not be in business, but you can still admire Bill Gates because of his philanthropic efforts. You might not like basketball, but you surely can appreciate Michael Jordan's dedication to the game.

When you choose a role model, choose an excellent human being overall, not just someone who is competent at their profession. Choose someone who is the best in your field if you want. Select multiple role models too. If you want to be the best, be sure to choose the best and ask them to mentor you. Take them out to a dinner. You can even pay them to coach you as previously mentioned. Ask them to speak in to your life. Become a student of this person who you admire and take notes on what you can do in your own life.

You can even send them a personal letter of encouragement and gratitude. If they are no longer living or old in age, try to study them as much as you can from their books or videos. Try to find some kind of artifacts that can help you learn more about them. You can even interview their family members to get a feel of how this person really was when they were living.

When you have a role model or several role models, you will be able to raise your standards and eventually raise you level of success. Study people who have done it before you. They had predecessors too. We become who we study and when people see, people do likewise. Don't be too surprised if your role model(s) let you down. I have met many of my own who were not who I thought they were. Just move on to the next one if this happens, regardless of how heart-shattering it can be. Having the right role models will give you The Ultimate Advantage!

Praise Everyone

One of the secrets to some of the most successful people is their ability to praise other people. Dale Carnegie once said in his book, 'How to Win Friends and Influence People' that people crave for praise all day long and you must be "Hearty in your approbation, and lavish in your praise." Everyone can use a good praise once in a while.

Be real in your praising. No one likes artificial praise or flattery. Most people can see straight through insincere praise if they have the discernment. Find something that you truly admire in someone. If they are wearing an outfit, there has to be a certain piece of clothing, accessory, or style about them that you really like. If you walk into someone's office, you will be sure to find some kind of artifact that you like and can relate to.

This is always a great conversation starter too. If you see someone with a book, you can simply ask them questions and complement the book for its bright colors.

A complement is an excellent to start a conversation with a stranger. Everyone has something that can be liked about them. Be sure to point it out and show them how much you admire them for it.

Mary Kay, the cosmetic queen, is known for managing her people with praise. This gave her employees high morale, which caused them to work harder on themselves and their jobs, thus producing higher results. Many business leaders try to find the good in what their employees do on and off the job. It is one of the biggest secrets to management. Many business leaders have praised their way to the top of their organization.

You can even use this in your family. Your spouse, children, and parents will always enjoy your encouraging words. The power of praise is so contagious that it will get people to open up to you in ways they would have never before. They will start disclosing covert information. Praising people for their differences will bring everyone together too. You sprinkle faith and encouragement on people when you praise them. Do this everywhere you go because it will give you The Ultimate Advantage!

Go Back to School

This may be abnormal advice, especially if you are an established professional, but it does have credence. Sometimes, you may need advanced course that will help you in your profession. A course on Human Resources, Theatre, or Business Writing can definitely help you make strides in your profession. Even courses like Geography and English Literature can give you a robust appetite for learning more in life.

College courses can help you learn fast in a systematic way. It doesn't always have to be for credit either. You can take a non-credit language courses on Spanish, French, or German. You can even take one on Yoga. If not college, you can go to another formal institution that will offer what you may desire. The Learning Annex and other training companies are a great example of this. If you commit to taking a course, this will be a major start on your advancement in life.

You can even go for an advanced degree, such as a masters or doctorate. You can go for specific designations, certificates, or licenses. Schools will give you what you need, according to your profession. Financial aid from the government or your job may be available too. Be sure to enroll into a school so that it can help you sharpen some skills in your life. This may be the secret for you in gaining The Ultimate Advantage!

Interview Children

Children are extraordinary characters, especially because of the faith and curiosity that they exemplify. When you talk to a child, you will find that many of them below the age of 12 will have a beginner's mind. Most of them are down for anything because they do not know of all of the consequences, whether good or bad.

Children have a special naiveté that most adults do not have. They have an unfailing imagination and believe that they can do anything. A child may hold 100 completely unrelated professions in their mind in one week and still be equally fascinated with each of them. They have no concept of failure and mistakes. There is nothing that can mentally stop them from doing a thing that they desire. Their unwavering faith is a force to be reckoned with, and one you should diligently study.

They also ask questions. Personal questions too. They ask questions like "why, when, where, who, what, and how" all of the time. They want to know everything. Their curiosity is like a foreigner before they first come to America, they want to know more, but they don't know what they want to know.

Children habitually experiment with even the little things. They count the ants on the sidewalk while adults step on them. They mix ingredients in their foods that adults would never imagine. They run in all directions purposelessly and fall down lifelessly on the grass that no adult would never fathom attempting.

Study and child and pick up some of their ways. You will be delighted by how much you will learn by a child. Their fascination and zeal toward life will help you expand your horizon and challenge you to think more creatively. In fact, you can even take your business or life problems to a child and explain it hypothetically. You will find out that their solution will probably be better than yours due to their simplicity of thinking. Some of the greatest businesspeople have solved their company's problem by listening to the simple, but profound advice of their young children.

These young creatures will certainly test your way of thinking when you choose to interview them. They will ask you person questions that may be more uncomfortable than you are willing to ask yourself. They are audacious on every level and will try anything, even if it is unreasonable. Talking to children will help you see more truth in your life and could even bring out the child in you. Speaking with children is part of The Ultimate Advantage!

Read a Grammar Book

Learning the proper grammar will give you the proper foundation in the words that you use. Often time, people will not use the right grammar and still not bother to know the difference. You use of language will determine how clearly you communicate your message to yourself and others.

Read a grammar book once in a while. If you consult with this great book once a week or even once a month, you will find a great increase in your level of thinking and your certainty in communication. Keep the grammar book around as you would a thesaurus or dictionary. Keep it right at hand near your desk and consult with it regularly.

Understanding the proper grammar will give you leverage in your language and help you manufacture better results as you communicate your message. It will remind you of what you learned in former schooling. Sometimes we cannot remember everything that we learned early on, but a good refresher is always good. Be sure not to correct people out loud when you do this activity as you realize your own development in your grammar. Just keep mental notes in your mind and realize that you are with people who are unwilling to learn what it takes to communicate effectively.

When you use the proper grammar, you will begin to realize other people who use the proper grammar. You will start to attract like-minded individuals, which will give you a stupendous and meteoric rise in life. This will help you to sort out the real and the artificial. When someone is telling you how successful they are, but you detect consistent flaws in their grammar, you will know the truth and the truth will set you free.

Forgive them for their lack of understanding and move on. Just know what you need to do and begin to work on your own language. Never condemn anyone because of their failure to use their language properly. Also, understand that certain dialects will affect people's use of grammar. Learn the proper grammar for your own good because it will give you The Ultimate Advantage!

If They Ask, Don't Join

For the rest of your life, people will always come to you and ask you to join their organization. They will ask you to become a board member of their company or an officer of some status in their club. They will tell you all of the benefits of joining their club. They will not tell you all of the burdens that come with joining their club. There are pros and cons to become a joiner.

Sometimes you will have mandatory meetings at inconvenient times. The meetings may become regimented, authoritative, and meaningless. The people in the group will tell you how great it is to be in this group and there is no other that parallels it in the world. They will create petty rules that will be almost impossible to break. You may even get the chance to make your own rules. If you do get the chance to make up an of the provisions or are largely involved in the group, you may still be stuck in the enormity of conformity.

Joining an organization for a good cause is always a good thing if it is for the right reason. However, most of the people in the group have not joined for the same reason you have. If you are to join a club of people, make sure that your commitment to it is short-term before committing long-term. Some people step into their first few meetings and blindly devote their lives to the group. Beware of the pitfalls of making such a decision. If possible, do not tell people how long you plan to stay with the group. They may pass on assignments to you that will make it almost impossible to leave the group.

The sad thing about why people join groups is because they were simply asked to join. It gave them an initial sense of belonging which only had an ephemeral effect. Some people join because they feel guilty. They may carry a false sense of fulfillment because they may feel more useful in their group than they do in their jobs, but it doesn't quite make them useful overall. Some groups will make you feel guilty because you may be the only one available to fulfill the role of the group at that particular time.

Instead of joining a group, you can keep your energy, creativity, and time to work on long-term personal projects. Joining a church, gym, or local club is a good thing if you want to have a steady foundation. If you want adventure with no strings attached, do not join more groups than you have to. You will miss the flexibility, unless the club is adventurous and mendable. If reasonable, stay away from groups if you plan to expand rapidly.

If you do join a group:

Be sure to visit a variety of groups; don't just settle for anyone your find. This may take extra time, but you will meet more people and build more relationships. If there is a group that is really attractive and is calling your name, then do join it. When you do join groups, do not only join it for the activities and/or the cause, but join it for the people. If you do not fit with the people, your commitment with the group will not be pleasant.

Join the group that will make you better. What will give you a greater edge is if you invent your group, like your mastermind, which was mentioned in an earlier part of this book. If you ever outgrow a group, which happens often, be sure to move on. Always surround yourself with people who will make you better. Let them be smarter and wiser than yourself. Search for the best group until you find one. Remember, you don't have to join the group. This will surely give you The Ultimate Advantage!

Pace Yourself with Intervals

Have you ever tried to work straight through the day? Did you ever realize what happens when you try to jam-pack everything into a 16-hour waking period? There tends to be utter failure. If you really know yourself, you would know that you can work diligently through a particular block of time.

For many, it is typically best to work in a 90 minute interval, and then take a 15-20 minute break at the end. Using this concentrated method will allow you to divert your focus under your own control. Usually, when a person tries to work more than 2 hours straight, they tend to lose focus and burn out.

Depending on who you are, what your needs are, and the intensity of your work, you should be able to produce meaningful work and also get 2-4 medium-sized tasks completed. You may also be able to knock out major projects in the process.

By working 90-minute time blocks into your day, consistently, you will be able to produce superior results. When you take your break, do not waste your time checking emails, social media, or random blogs and commentary. Rather, take the time to take a walk, have a snack, or get into an intellectual conversation with yourself or another person.

Use this time management system and give yourself adequate breaks. Celebrate when appropriate and do not try to overload yourself. Pace yourself throughout the day with these intervals and you should be able to have the best week every week. No more mediocre weeks. No more time wasters. No more zone-outs on non-related production. Get the best out of your day, but do not let your day get the best out of you.

Here are other working intervals:

1. 30-45 minutes productivity with a 5-10 minute break
    *for hyper people
2. 60-75 minutes productivity with a 10-15 minute break

3. 90-120 minutes productivity with a 20 minute break
4. 180 minutes productivity with a 30-45 minute break
    *Only if you can get away with it
    **No more than 2 times per day

You can always mix up these intervals throughout the day. Use a perfect blend and plan your day out the night before. Remember the 5 P's-Proper Planning Prevents Poor Performance. Enjoy your masterpiece because pacing yourself with intervals will give you The Ultimate Advantage!

Do What You Say You Will Do

Have you ever ran into a person who promises that they will deliver, but you find that they never came through? How does it make you feel? What about a person who says they will call you, but they never do? Maybe they may have told you that they would make a special connection for you? It has probably happen dozens of times, right?

Integrity is doing what you say you will do. It is being who you say that you are. Many people will go around acting like they can provide in ways that they cannot. They speak in pompous and circuitous terms. They even look you in the eyes with conviction and tell you in the most dramatic way that they will deliver. When you look for their follow-up, you find they did not deliver what they said they would.

You may know that there is always a different kind of person. It is the person who under-promises and over-delivers. This is the person with the highest regard for humanity. This person has integrity like no other because they are being who they say they will be.

Is this you? Are you the kind of person to adhere to moral character and live the most ethical life? If you are committed to this, you will have many friends and a steady life. Even if you consider yourself an average person, you are not if you have integrity. These people are as hard to find DMW without a waiting line!

When you do what you say you will do, you will have respect from both friends and enemies. It is the closest way of pursuing perfection. You are basically obeying yourself and others while you serve in a cheerful way. Your credibility is all you have. Your reputation and integrity is your best advertisement. Treat your integrity like a sacred gift. Having high integrity must be practiced. When you have this attribute, it will give you The Ultimate Advantage!

Time, Energy, and Money

Creativity can be gained or lost depending on how we use our time, energy, and money. When you know how to use these three resources, you will become unstoppable and you will have control over almost every aspect of your life.

You only have a particular amount of time, energy, and money in a day. It must be used wisely. It must all be well-balanced. For instance, if you try to take too much time trying to avoid the toll on the highway, you may save $2, but you lost 20 minutes and brainpower in learning how to do it. For the sake of money alone, you helped yourself, but you lost your time and energy.

If you have some money, but want more money and decide to put all of your energy and time into working overtime in manual labor jobs, you will find that you will end up right where you began, because you will have no time and energy left at the end of the day.

What if you had all the time and money in the world? You will find yourself using all of your energy searching for creative ways to use it. Your time and money can go in good or bad ways, depending on how you use it. If you had all money, but little time and energy, your money may be worthless too, unless you use it in the proper way.

As you can tell, there are many more variables that can be plugged into this equation. How do you use your time, energy, and money? You have access to all of these key resources, but how well you use it will determine your level of success. By the way, time is the most valuable of these three because you can never gain it again. Time is not money. Time is more valuable than money. Forget the old adage that 'time is money' If you use these three elements correctly, especially time, you will have The Ultimate Advantage!

Live with No Regrets

It is true that when most people reach a certain age, they start to regret the things they did not do. In fact, if you ask most senior citizens what they would change if they were young again, they would tell you to 'take more risks'.

Regret is worse than failure. Sometimes we are afraid to fail because it may make us lose face. Does it really matter? If we fail, so what? Most people never even try because they are surrounded by people who do not support or understand the risk that they think about taking. Elbert Hubbard said, "The greatest mistake you can make in life is to be continually fearing you will make a mistake." People go to the graves everyday full of deep regret, wishing that they could have done what they knew they should have done.

If you take a risk on what you truly believe in, it will most likely work out. Is there something that you have been thinking about that you know you should start working on? Is there a special project that you must undertake before your life is over? Go out and do it! Try to ask the question, "What if?" What if you made it work? What if you were a smashing success?

When you ask this question, it will force you to come up with creative solutions that can revolutionize your thinking. What if you started thinking more about your successes than your failures? You will be surprised with how many obstacles you will be able to break through by asking this question. There may be obstacles that disappear, or quite frankly, never even appear to begin with!

When you live a life of no regret, you will experience a higher level of satisfaction. You will be able to go places you never thought you will go. You will become much wiser because you trust yourself and your actions. You will truly become the person you want to be. When you live with no regrets, you will have The Ultimate Advantage!

The 20 Idea Method

People do not run out of money. Instead, they run out of ideas. Think about how far you can go if your actually write your ideas down. Imagine if you wrote them down every day! Right now, you will learn a very powerful method that can dramatically influence every part of your life.

Every day when you wake up, you can break out a sheet of paper and write down on the top of the page one of your major goals for the year. After you write your major goal down, create all of the ideas that you can come up with. By the time you reach 20 ideas, something magical usually happens. Do not be concerned with the quality of your ideas, just write them down.

This method is by-far the greatest method of brainstorming for you to use. It forces you to think and trains you to take action on your ideas. You will be able to come up with ideas you never even knew you had! This activity will take you to great depths and help you research topics that did not come to your mind before you wrote them down. This timeless method is so valuable and easy to do.

Imagine sitting down for 10-15 minutes each day and writing down all of your ideas to reach your goals. You can even use this to solve major challenges in your life. You can propose your challenge or goal as a question and brainstorm your way into an answer. It is a marvelous way to overcome problems and obstacles. This method will work for you. It doesn't matter who you are or what profession you are in. Try it!

If you did this 5 days per week for a year, or 50 weeks (with 2 weeks off), you can generate over 5,000 ideas per year! Imagine what you can do in 10 years!! You will come up with 50,000 ideas in a decade. You can bet that at least 10% of them are actionable.

Let's break this down mathematically:

20 ideas X 5 days per week=100 ideas per week

100 ideas per week X 50 weeks per year=5,000 ideas per year

5,000 ideas per year X 10 years=50,000 ideas in 10 years

50,000 ideas X 45 years (average entire working life) =2,250,000

How many ideas do you have? All you really need is one that can be developed over time. Are you letting your ideas go to waste? Try a new goal or challenge every day and watch how many solutions you come up with. It only takes one solid idea to make a fortune! This method alone is worth the price of this book. It will definitely give you The Ultimate Advantage!

Asking for Help

Have you ever needed help before? You are a human that may be good at several things, but you are not good at everything. You may be a conservative, but you need a liberal opinion once in a while. You might be very traditional, but you can always hire a new school person to develop a website for you. If are not good at waking up early and getting started, ask someone to call you to motivate you. You can ask for things in prayer too.

Asking is a sign of strength. If you can ask, it shows that you are going to need help. Help is on the way. A weak person is full of pride and is afraid to ask for help because they may feel that it is simply too much to ask for something. They feel that they must learn everything. If you feel that you must learn everything, you will be what most people call a 'jack of all trades'. They never quite get anywhere because they do everything themselves and have not really become good at something.

If you are going to build a foundation, build it with the proper help. No castle is constructed alone. You cannot make a masterpiece or build a city by yourself. Every artisan needs a hand to complete their work. Be sure to reach out in time of need. You will be surprised what kind of services can be supplied. You will be even more surprised by who needs your help. Asking for help will give you The Ultimate Advantage!

Paying the Price

Paying the price requires full heart. There are two positions in life:

1. Playing Now and Paying Later
2. Paying Now and Playing Later

Playing Now and Paying Later

You have many peers who are wasting time right now. They may be at the coffee shop gossiping, sitting at home watching Facebook pictures, or making their regular runs with the negative news or ESPN highlights. This is not the best way to use their time. What they will find later in life is that there are many things that they could have done better earlier on in life. When they reach their 40's, 50's, 60's, 70's, and 80's, they will not have the life that they want. They won't be able to support their favorite charities, drive that brand new red convertible they always wanted, or even buy the right gifts for their grandchildren.

Because they waited all of these years, they find themselves in a difficult situation. When they were young, they enjoyed life and did the things that gave them the gratification at that time. What they failed to realize is that life exacts a price. If you wait too long, the price is higher because of the exorbitant interest. It's like having a credit card, if you don't pay your dues, it adds up quickly and you will find yourself trying to dig yourself out of a hole that you have created. Everyone wants to live long, but no one wants to get old. Getting old is a choice that you make. When you refuse to pay the price, you will get old.

Paying Now and Playing Later

This alternative is better. You may be embarking on a new journey. Don't concern yourself if you believe if you are too young or too old. Once you decide to start paying the price, you will see the benefits within the first few months. If you are willing to read the books, attend the seminars, set powerful goals, make many mistakes along the way, and develop yourself, you will find in 5-10 years from your starting date, you will be right exactly where you wanted to be. It will take 20 years even if you have major mental or physical handicaps. Best of all, it can be done more than once in a lifetime.

For example, Arnold Schwarzenegger accomplished several major things in his life. He was a businessman, body-builder, actor, politician, and author. Bruce Lee mastered ping pong, fighting, acting, and other activities before he died at age 32. There are many examples of people who accomplished different levels of success within one lifetime.

When you pay the price early on, you will be able to enjoy ample benefits that await you. You will see that beautiful house that you have always imagined. You will prosper immeasurably in every area of your life. You may even extend your life because of the total commitment and fulfillment of living. When you pay the price early on, you will be able to play later in life, without reservations. There will be no limitations on what you can achieve. You can be productive well into your 90's like Norman Vincent Peale, Peter Drucker, Billy

Graham, Nelson Mandela, and Ronald Reagan. When you pay the price all of your life, you will be the best person you can possibly be. Paying the price will give you The Ultimate Advantage!

How to deal with your Enemies

You will be confronted by your enemies many times in your life. You may have an enemy at any given time of your life. You may even have several operating at once. They often come when you are doing your best work. It is their duty to keep you from being your very best. Sun Tzu said "Know your enemy and know yourself and you can fight a hundred battles without disaster."

Enemies come in all shapes and sizes. They may attack with hate, jealousy, lust, greed, discouragement, ignorance, physical obstructions, or they may simply be time-wasters. They will distract you from your goals if you do not recognize them. Stay away from any types of arguments and negativity. Don't feel that you have to answer to anyone.

You can find approval in your own sense of being. People will make derogatory remarks and talk bad about you. There is nothing that you can do. People will criticize you and even ostracize you for doing the good work that you do. These people can be the closest people in your life. The more successful you are, the more enemies you will have. What's funny is that your enemies will sometimes support you to make it seem like they are on your side, but they are just curious about what you are doing. Some enemies try to get close to you so that they can steal your methods. Don't let this happen, especially if you have something that no one can offer.

The best way to battle your adversaries is to not put up a fight. These nitpicker and small-brainers will do whatever it takes to get on your nerves, only if you let them. Ignore them completely and acquiesce every time you are in the midst of an attack, especially if it makes no sense. Martin Luther King Jr. said "Love is the only force capable of transforming an enemy into a friend."

Most attacks have no validation or reason for their existence. Treat everyone, especially enemies, in the highest regard and be very sensitive to their needs, even if their demands are unrealistic. Show your support and show more kindness to them. Love and kindness are the best ways to disarm your enemies.

Always forgive your adversaries. Do not even act like anything happened. Be completely blameless in your life. All they want is your attention. If you waste it on them, you cannot focus on your goals. All you have to do is forgive them for their lack of understanding. John F. Kennedy said, "Forgive your enemies, but never forget their names."

Most of your attacks will be because of your spiritual growth. Be sure to love your enemies. Don't let your opposition discourage you or keep you from reaching your potential. When it comes down to it, you can be your own biggest enemy. Convert your enemies into your friends. Forgiveness is your best revenge on those who persecute you. Loving and forgiving your enemies will give you The Ultimate Advantage!

Do What Needs To Be Done

Even if you don't feel like doing it, certain things must be done. It may be the little things that spring up. Make sure they get done. You may sometimes struggle with keeping your desk clean, but sometimes you have to clear it off and make room for your priorities. Same thing with your car!

You may have a spouse waiting at home that needs your attention. Even though you may pass the flower shop everyday home from work, it doesn't mean you cannot buy him or her roses. Maybe there are some techniques that you learned in this book that you know must be implemented. You may have delayed because you said you would get to it later, but the time is now. When you procrastinate, you lose the most essential asset, time. Get on the ball and do what you know needs to be done, even if you do not feel like doing it. Neglect is the biggest sin. It also leads to poverty, confusion, and frustrations.

It may be challenging to do the trivial things at your work, but you know how much satisfaction it will give you once it is done. Sometimes little tasks can be knocked out quickly if you put it on your to-do list. When it comes to big tasks, you can set a block of time and get it done. You will find that the flow and momentum of doing it will drive you to get it done, even though you didn't feel like doing it in the first place. Only average people skip what needs to be done. Superior people get it done no matter what.

Doing what needs to be done is important because it forbids sloppiness. You clean up after yourself by taking the extra steps to force yourself to believe that what you are doing will provide fulfillment and a job well done. When you do what needs to be done, when it needs to be done, this will give you The Ultimate Advantage.

Questions

A question is one of the most important learning tools that you can use. It forces you to think in different ways. Questions can help you reveal the deepest level of thinking in your mind. It can help erase bad habits and completely renew your way of reasoning. Asking the right questions can change your life dramatically. They should be developed and thought of every day.

Many people ask the question, "What's wrong with you?" instead of "What can I do to help you?" They may even ask, "Why don't I get it?" instead of "What can I do to understand this better?" People too often conclude on their questions. Don't answer your questions, but question your answers. Question where your questions are taking you. Foolish people look for answers, wise people look for questions.

Questioning Yourself

Questions help you search within your heart and mind. They are excellent tools to help you make surveys on anything you can possibly know. You can always ask questions in your mind such as, "Where can I find my next best cookbook?" or "What is the best use of my time right now?" The more specific your questions are, the more likely they will be able to take you to where you need to be.

It often appears that undeveloped people have all the answers, while developed people have all of the questions. Too often, we assume that things are the way they are without checking in with a question that can revolutionize our reasoning. Questions are challenging to ask because they expose us to new truths that we may feel we are not ready for. Questions lead us to truth.

Use questions in reflection. At the end of the day, ask yourself "What did I do today that went very well?" Also ask, "If I had to do my day all over again, what would I change and why?" These questions can change your life in the next 30-60 days.

Questioning Others

You can also use questions for open-ended questions. Instead of asking, "Is this all you have in this store?" you can ask, "What more do you have available?" The first question can sound insulting, but the second question sounds complementary. Instead of asking, "Did you like the movie?" you can ask, "What was your favorite scene of the movie?" If you get people to talk about a subject, they will eventually start talking about themselves, and you can learn a lot from them. The first question can usually lead to a 'yes' or a 'no', which doesn't take you anywhere and gives room for the other person to ask questions.

You can also use questions effectively before your prepare for a meeting or a phone call. To best serve yourself and others, prepare 5-10 questions for a 30-60 minute phone call or meeting. The more questions you prepare, the better it would be. Not every question will be answered the way you would like, nor will all questions be asked. You can always work your questions into each conversation you have to your advantage.

Questions help satisfy your deep curiosity. All humans are highly curious and questions can give us a glimpse into more of what is unknown. The specificity of your questions will also build credibility. Asking questions will also give you power because it forces the other person to talk. Always get yourself and other people on your side by the questions that you use. Great questions lead to great intelligence. Asking the right questions will give you The Ultimate Advantage.

Timing is Everything

For many activities that you do, you should know the time it takes to get done. For instance, you should know how quickly you can get a certain meal done. You should know how long it will take to take a shower. You should be able to know how soon you can finish the book you are currently working on.

Creating a measurement system is actually easier than you think. All you need is a stopwatch. Time yourself so that you can better plan and coordinate your activities. When you know the time of a particular task, you will know how to slow down or speed up. This will give you more control too.

You should time your meetings and meals. Everything should be timed. You may think that it takes 20 minutes to eat your meal, but it may actually take 40 minutes. You may think that the time you take at the gym is 1 hour instead of your actual time of 2 hours. Sometimes certain things aren't taken into account such as transportation, preparation, conversations, and any other logistics. A timer can certainly help you realize what can be added or subtracted to your habits as you use exact measures.

By keeping time systematically, you will gain more control of your life and be able to fit in certain tasks faster than you believe. If you think in terms of time, it is the highest level of thinking possible because time cannot be gained again. When you keep time, this will surely give you The Ultimate Advantage!

Mind-Mapping

Mind-mapping is one of the best ways to capture your thoughts while bringing them to physical form. Mind maps helps you build your memory, expand your creativity, and solve problems more effectively. You can also type in "Mind-Mapping" in Google and you will find thousands of examples.

Here is how it is done:

1. Start in the center of a blank page with no lines turned sideways. Starting in the center gives your brain freedom to stretch your mind and think more creatively.

2. Use a picture or image in the middle to stimulate your imagination. You can also use a word, question, or idea.

3. Use colored pencils or pens to draw more attention to your mind. Color adds more vibrancy

to your Mind-Map. Color will also intensify your Mind-Map.

4. Connect your main branches to the central image and connect your second and third-level branches to the first and second levels, etc. Do this because your brain works by association. It likes to link two (or three, or four) things together. If you connect the branches, you will understand, comprehend, and remember much more

5. Make your branches curved rather than straight-lined. Do this because straight lines is boring to your brain.

6. Use one key word for each line. Single key words give your Mind-Map more power and flexibility.

7. Use images throughout your Mind-Map. With each image, like the central image, is also worth a thousand words. If you have only 10 images in your Mind Map, it is already the equal of 10,000 words of notes!

Mind-mapping will help you put ideas together faster than ever. It will help you remember speeches and goals. Create your own formula for success by using this strategic method. Use this powerful tool as you gain The Ultimate Advantage!

Create Value

Many people will work according to the hours in any given week. They measure their contribution by hours instead of value. If you focus on creating value, you will not have to focus on how many hours you put in a particular job.

There are hundreds of millions of people who are working according to the clock. They rush out when they boss tells them they are done, but do they truly create value? Are they committed to doing the best job or are they just waiting for a paycheck for their survival? We can choose to be secure or we can choose to pursue growth. True growth will allow us to create value for others around us.

Does your neighbor need your help with landscaping or any odd jobs? Creating value doesn't always have to pay. It can be as simple as a helping hand. Too many people make the trite remark "It is not my job", as if it is as belaboring as the menial tasks that they do at work.

It is too unfortunate that people are not willing to

look at their contributions and how it can be increased. One way of thinking about creating value is by asking the simple question, "Do I find myself helpful?" If you feel that this question is challenging to answer, it is time to look for something that will make you deliver more value.

Try to deliver more value in everything you do. If you find that something isn't worth doing, cut it out of your schedule and search for a more meaningful task. It is not the hours you put in, but what you put in the hours. Put the most into your hours. Creating value will pay off in dividends, help you grow into fulfillment, and give you The Ultimate Advantage!

Imagination is Everything

There are so many things that can be created in the mind. Here you have the chance to choose what thought you want to have. In this mental factory, you will be able to see into the future and dream the biggest dreams.

Your imagination can help you create the environment that you have always longed for. It can stimulate your senses and take you places in your mind. Use your imagination to construct all things that are favorable. Eject any ideas in your imagination that debilitates you in any way. Your imagination should only help you reach your intended desires.

Create a mental picture of what you desire in your mind and hold it for as long as possible. See the details and experience the ambiance of what you imagine. Go through the experience in your mind. Many of the most successful people prepare by visualization. You are more likely to climb Mount Everest if you can visualize it first.

Without a vision, we would not exist. Everything around you was created by the imagination of others.

Great works have art have been created due to the faculty of imagination. Tall skyscrapers, music, and museums only exist because someone used their imagination.

What do you do with your imagination? Do you use it to follow your dreams? Do you see yourself doing great things and accomplishing great feats? Create an empire with your imagination and think as far out as you can. If you can see as far as you can go, you will go as far as you can see. Using your imagination will give you The Ultimate Advantage!

Conclusion

Now you have what it takes to gain The Ultimate Advantage in life. Although there were many suggestions, you will be able to use them to get promoted in all levels of life. This comprehensive book should have made you think about all of the new tools that you can use to pursue mastery in everything you undertake.

If you decide to use a dozen or more of these tips in the process of reading this book, you will do very well for yourself. Revisit many of them to get some new ideas on how you can take a more strategic approach in your life. Be sure to teach these techniques to the people around you and lend them a copy of this book. They will be glad if you did.

Go ahead and make the changes necessary to achieve more in life. Follow your dreams and get what you always wanted out of life. You have everything you need to make a difference. What's more, you have The Ultimate Advantage!

ABOUT THE AUTHOR

Daniel Ally is a highly-demanded Thought Leader, Author, and a Business Growth Expert who has transformed thousands of people to reach their desired personal and business goals. Today, he is the Founder and CEO of The Ally Way International, a consulting firm, and has worked with various clients ranging from Fortune 500 companies to independently-owned workshops.

He also runs his subsidiary business called Dignify Designs, which is a fully-functioning branding agency. Dignify Designs primarily focuses on websites and book publishing, but takes on special projects as well. Daniel also coaches aspiring speakers to help them learn more about the professional speaking industry.

Daniel is the author of his first book, "You Are the Boss!" Daniel's hobbies include reading the Bible, traveling, speaking, and exercising. Daniel is a devoted follower of Jesus Christ and alludes all of his success to following Him.

www.danielally.com

The Ultimate Advantage

Mark 9:23

Made in the USA
Middletown, DE
27 January 2015